The Art & Science of Coaching Series

COACHING FOOTBALL'S SPREAD OFFENSE

Tim Stowers
Barry Butzer

COACHES CHOICE

©1998 Coaches Choice Books. All rights reserved. Printed in the United States.

No part of this book may be reproduced, stored in a retrieval system, or transmitted, in any form or by any means, electronic, mechanical, photocopying, recording, or otherwise, without the prior permission of Sagamore Publishing, Inc.

ISBN: 1-57167-161-7
Library of Congress Catalog Card Number: 97-68314

Cover Design and Diagrams: Deborah M. Bellaire
Cover Photos: Front Cover—Courtesy of Georgia Southern University
Production Manager: Michelle Summers

Coaches Choice Books is a division of: Sagamore Publishing, Inc.
P.O. Box 647
Champaign, IL 61824-0647
Web Site: http//www.sagamorepub.com

DEDICATION

This book is dedicated to all those football coaches who coach for the right reasons. To coach and prepare their teams to be the best they can possibly be on game day and to ensure that their players earn their degrees, so that when they go out into the real world they can be positive influences on society.

ACKNOWLEDGMENTS

During the course of writing the book on the Spread Offense, one individual went above and beyond the call of duty in order to ensure it went to print. This book could not have become a reality without the effort and dedication of Coach Barry Butzer.

T.S.

I would like to thank Coach Tim Stowers for the opportunity to co-author this book with him and Jim Peterson for recommending me to Tim.

I would also like to thank my wife, Nancy, who has stood faithfully on the sidelines for 35 years, and our son, Scott, who sometimes had to play second fiddle to guys in hard hats (football helmets or Army steel pots). Thanks to my mother, Mrs. Albert (Naomi King) Hess and the entire King family, who taught me that hard work and discipline always pay off. To my father and stepmother, Peg and "Chap" Butzer of Nevada, and the Butzer clan in Pennsylvania, thank you for all your support.

B.B.

CONTENTS

Dedication 3

Acknowledgments 4

Foreword 6

Preface 7

Chapter

1   Coaching in the 90s 9

2   Why the Spread? 13

3   The Bread and Butter 17

4   The Zone Dive 29

5   The Trap 33

6   The Trap Option 39

7   The Speed Option 47

8   The Play-Action Pass 53

9   Sprint-Out Pass 63

10 Knocking it in the Zone 73

11 Secondary and Special Plays 81

12 Football Graffiti 91

     About the Authors 96

FOREWORD

After having coached, coached with, and coached against Tim Stowers; I feel that I have a thorough understanding of his offensive approach, strategy, and coaching philosophy. His coaching record speaks for itself. I have seen Coach Stowers' Spread Offense up close and personal on several occasions. It is a simple attack to run, but a complex one to defend. The Spread Offense does exactly what its name implies—it spreads the defense horizontally with the option game and vertically with four quick receivers at the line of scrimmage. Unlike the wishbone, a defense cannot overcommit the secondary to stop the run. If you do, you are opening yourself up for the homerun via the play action pass. The Spread Offense presents a balanced formation, which dictates a balanced defensive alignment. This offensive attack allows a team to move the ball against superior personnel, because it is not necessary to block all the defenders. The speed element of the Spread Offense is extremely difficult to simulate in practice, therefore causing problems with defensive preparation. Furthermore, it is hard to prepare a defense to play option responsibility and get ready for the Spread Offense in one week. This versatility puts opposing defensive teams at a disadvantage.

I highly recommend *Coaching Football's Spread Offense* for both college and high school offenses. Once again, it is easy to implement, but difficult to stop. Coach Stower's expertise with the Spread Offense is second to none in the coaching profession. He has had the opportunity to be involved with the Spread Offense through four NCAA I-AA National Titles and one Southern Conference Championship at Georgia Southern University. I know you will find this book to be a very helpful aid in your research of the Spread Offensive System.

Coach Larry Blakeney
Head Football Coach
Troy State University

PREFACE

After having coached college football for 18 years, I have learned that football is an ever changing game. Coaches are always searching for something that may give them an edge for the upcoming season. This book on the Spread Offense is intended to help lay the foundation for those coaches wanting to employ this offense or give a coaching staff who is already running it some valuable information. Many times a coaching staff will go to a clinic, read a book or article and will hear one concept that is in line with their current pattern of preparation. Often times that concept can be a turning point in their direction or path for the upcoming season. It is my hope that as you read this book you gain an edge somewhere between the front cover or back cover that enables your staff and team to be more successful in the upcoming football season.

Tim Stowers
Former Head Football Coach
Georgia Southern University

CHAPTER 1

Coaching in the 90s

It has been stated that all coaching is dealing with a series of crises. How a coach responds to each crisis will usually dictate his tenure. The 90s coach wears many hats and is ultimately responsible for everything that occurs in the program, whether it involves coaching, counseling, marketing, salesmanship, or public relations. Therefore, a coach must establish a basic coaching philosophy. The Roots of the Team is an example of a basic philosophy on which a program can be built.

Roots of the Team

KISS

Keep It Simple Stupid, or KISS, can be characterized by stating that the only thing better than a simple idea is an even simpler one. If a coach tries to run "football's twenty best plays" from every formation in football, he has availability, not specificity. His players will be thinking on the run rather than reacting on the run. When an offense is based on five basic running plays, a coach can achieve specificity by performing numerous repetitions of those plays. A company in California studied sports skills and found that to become familiar with a skill, an athlete must perform that skill 250,000 times. To perfect that skill, the athlete must perform it almost 1,000,000 times. Try to imagine how many times Mary Lou Retton performed her vault to achieve that perfect 10 in the 1984 Olympic games. In football, a team may only have time to practice a skill 250 times to become familiar with it, and 1,000 times to perfect it. A coach cannot achieve perfection by running "football's twenty best plays" from every formation in football. If a coach narrows his focus and applies the KISS principle, he may find that his team can achieve near-perfection through repetition.

GATA

Using the GATA (Go After Them Aggressively) principle, a defensive football player's value to his team can be measured by how far he is from the ball at the end of each play. The average football play lasts a total of five seconds. If a player takes part in 70 plays per game, he has participated in 5.8 minutes of football. Over the course of an 11-game season, that adds up to 63.8 minutes of football. Taking into consideration the ratio of practice opportunities to games, approximately 15 to 1, it is inexcusable for a player not to "GATA" for 5.8 minutes per game.

Zero Defects
Zero defects is an old Army term that applies perfectly to the kicking game. The kicking game is important for two reasons. First, it equals about one third of a football game. Second, three of the biggest plays in a football game that can swing the momentum from one team to the other involve the kicking game:

1. A blocked punt for a touchdown.
2. A kick-off return for a touchdown.
3. A punt return for a touchdown.

Any of these can sap the "will to win" out of an opponent. Therefore, an EDGE period (Extra Determination, Guts, and Effort) is established in the middle of practice, not at the end of practice, to emphasize the kicking game. One or two phases of the kicking game should be carefully planned for 10 to 15 minutes and worked in during the middle of each practice. This will help prevent defects in the kicking game and give a football team an EDGE in close games.

Do Right
Do Right applies to every aspect of the team and the program. Some coaches give handouts or booklets with long lists of rules to follow, which the players take back to their rooms to collect dust. In life, as in football, the series of decisions a person makes during his lifetime will either fall into the category of doing right or doing wrong. There is no gray area. A gray area provides a deep dark hole in which no one has fault or responsibility. One of the most important concepts young people must learn is responsibility. A person should either do right or accept the responsibility for doing wrong and do it right the next time.

Study Hard and Say No
The reason for going to college is to study, earn a degree, and build a strong academic background upon which to build a lifelong education. At most, only five percent of all college football players go on to make six-figure salaries in the NFL. Imagine a player studying one evening for a test which will decide his eligibility for the upcoming fall. A teammate who had the same teacher for the same class walks in and says, "You don't need to cram for that test. I had that teacher before and he likes athletes, so you don't need to pull an all-nighter. Come with me to this party. A girl in one of my classes is going to be there, and she's dying to meet you." Will that player be strong enough to say no? It takes moral courage and discipline to simply say no.

Attitude
Some people see a glass of water and say it's half full. Some see it and say it's half empty. A person is either an eternal optimist or an eternal pessimist. People can

detect a positive attitude without a word being spoken. As an example, look at the phrase "opportunityisnowhere." It can be read either as "opportunity is now here" or "opportunity is nowhere." If two players, one with a superior attitude and one with a poor attitude, do the same workout for a period of six weeks, the player with the superior attitude will become bigger, faster, and stronger. A person should live his life with a great attitude. If he does not, he is taking up space where someone else could excel.

Any program that employs the Roots of the Team—the KISS principle, the GATA principle, zero defects, doing right, studying hard and saying no, and having a positive attitude—will produce players and team records that are winners both on and off the football field.

CHAPTER 2

Why the Spread?

A great coach once said that "good football teams either do something different or they do it better." The Spread formation (Diagram 2-1) gives teams a chance to do both. It is a hybrid formation, a combination of the Run and Shoot (even though no Run and Shoot base plays are employed) and the Flexbone. This formation gives an offense the capability, by alignment, to stretch a defense both horizontally and vertically. The Spread stretches the defense horizontally with the simultaneous threat of various double and triple options and vertically by placing four quick receivers at the line of scrimmage (LOS). The end result is that the Spread formation dictates, by its alignment, a balanced response from the defense. They cannot afford to "gang up" on the running game. With four quick receivers at or near the LOS, the defense must also respect the pass or face the consequences.

SPREAD FORMATION

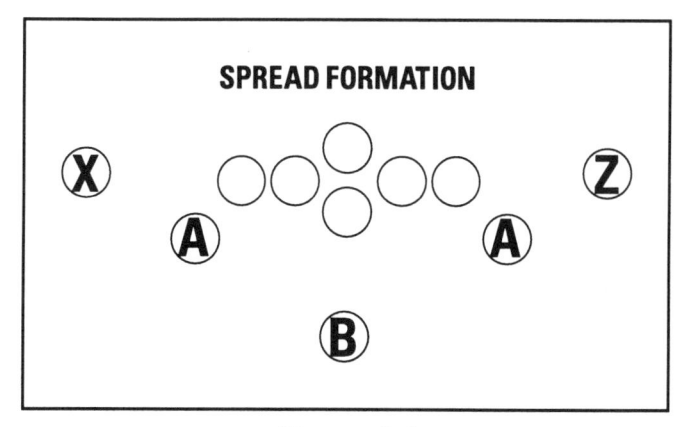

Diagram 2-1

Alignment

The two wide receivers, X and Z, line up near the numbers. Their exact location depends on where the ball is located. They assume a two-point stance with X on the left and Z on the right. The A-backs line up with their inside foot three feet outside and one foot behind the tackle's hip. The A-backs use a staggered two-point stance with the inside foot back. This stance allows them to go in motion prior to the snap, thus allowing the offense to gain a numbers advantage before the defense can adjust. (This A-back motion, called tail motion, is shown in Diagram 2-

2.) Tail motion is achieved by using a rhythmic snap count which allows the backside A-back to take 1 to 1.5 steps before the ball is snapped. The A-back's path is through the heels of the B-back. He continues to stay in pitch relationship to the quarterback (4.5 to 5 yards off the quarterback's hip).

TAIL MOTION

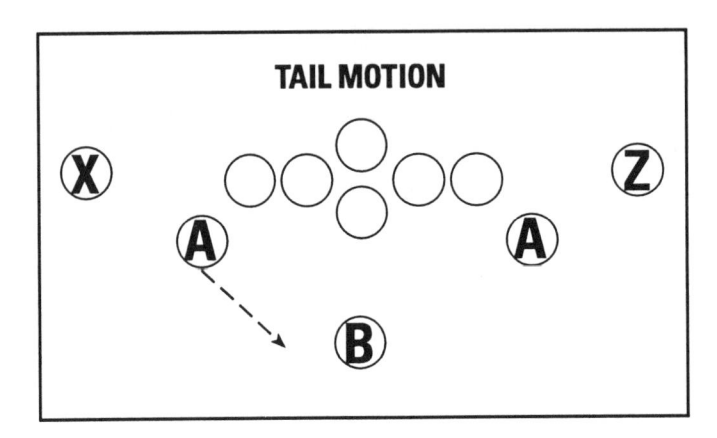

Diagram 2-2

The B-back uses a three-point stance. He lines up directly behind the quarterback with his heels five yards behind the front tip of the football. It is important to remember that a spread B-back is not a wishbone fullback, but a tailback. He must be both a solid inside runner and a perimeter runner.

The offensive line uses a three-point stance with three foot splits across the front. The linemen's stance is toe-to-instep or parallel, with enough weight forward so that forward movement occurs when the grounded hand is moved. The guards and tackles line up behind the ball with their ear even with the center's beltline. This alignment gives the guards and tackles an advantage for the pulling and zone blocking required by the Spread offense. The three foot split is the maximum width from which the linemen can be effective on the backside scoop block. The three-point stance has also proven to be most effective for the pulling and zone blocking required by this offensive system.

There are five basic runs that are featured from the Spread formation:

- The Zone Dive
- The Trap
- The Triple Option
- The Trap Option
- The Speed Option

Each of these plays is discussed in detail in subsequent chapters. These plays are designed to be run against almost any defensive front. The passing game consists of play action and sprint out passes. The KISS principle is applied to both the offensive scheme or game plan and the on-the-field preparation. For example, these five basic running plays are repeatedly practiced against the four or five defenses that an offensive team sees on a weekly basis. The key is repetition—working known plays into the offense, not putting in new plays. This philosophy gives the Spread formation the advantage of executing the five base plays better than the opposing team can execute its defense against those plays. By alignment, the Spread formation requires that the defense defend the entire field. It also gives an offensive team the chance to move the football against sometimes superior defensive personnel, because the option can be used to eliminate defenders without having to block them.

The five-play structure is the bread and butter of the Spread attack. Nevertheless, a team should also have two or three secondary runs and a few special plays (reverses, halfback passes, etc.) in each of its battle plans. The five base plays are carried in the offensive game plan every week. Secondary running plays and special plays may vary from week to week based upon film study.

CHAPTER 3

The Bread and Butter

The one base play in the Spread attack that can always be counted on should be the triple option. When all else fails, the triple option is the play an option team should be able to go to. In order to be successful at the triple option, at least two of the three phases (give, keep, and pitch) have to be effective. One advantage of this offense is the fact that a team can get by with a quarterback with average athletic ability if he has good decision-making skills. A team in this situation would lean toward the give or pitch triple-option attack. However, it is best to have the strength of the triple option at the B-back and quarterback positions. The most successful Spread offense quarterbacks have not necessarily had great speed, but rather an ability to make defenders miss tackles. An option team becomes most potent when all three phases of the triple option are effective.

For communication purposes, it is imperative that the quarterback, the B-back, and the offensive linemen become familiar with the various places in which a defensive lineman can align. The whereabouts of the defenders have to be communicated and understood in a game situation in order for the offensive assignments to be properly carried out. The numbering system, gap calls, and defensive techniques used in this book are shown in Diagram 3-1.

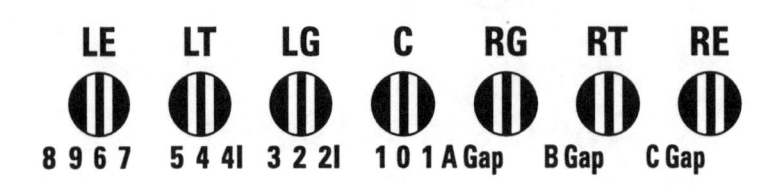

```
        LE    LT    LG    C    RG    RT    RE
        ⓘ    ⓘ    ⓘ    ⓘ    ⓘ    ⓘ    ⓘ
       8 9 6 7  5 4 4I  3 2 2I  1 0 1 A Gap   B Gap   C Gap
```

Diagram 3-1

LE—Left End
LT—Left Tackle
LG—Left Guard
C—Center

RG—Right Guard
RT—Right Tackle
RE—Right End

"0" Technique   Head-up on the center, responsible for the physical playside A Gap or backside A Gap.
"1" Technique   Outside eye to outside shoulder of the center. Also called a shade technique with A Gap responsibility.
"2i" Technique   Inside eye to inside shoulder the guard, A Gap responsibility.
"2" Technique   Head-up on the guard in a pre-slant alignment, A Gap responsibility.
"3" Technique   Outside eye to inside shoulder of the guard, B Gap responsibility.
"4i" Technique   Inside eye to inside shoulder of the guard, with B Gap responsibility.
"4" Technique   Head-up on the tackle in a pre-slant alignment, B Gap responsibility.
"5" Technique   Outside eye to outside shoulder of the tackle, C Gap responsibility.
"6" Technique   Head-up on the tight end in a pre-slant alignment, with C Gap responsibility.
"7" Technique   Inside eye to inside shoulder of the tight end, with C Gap responsibility.
"8" Technique   On L.O.S. outside the tackle in a hip position, or walked off, halfway between the tackle and the wide out.
"9" Technique   Outside eye to outside shoulder of the tight end, contain responsibility.

The Mesh

The connection of the quarterback and the B-back is called the mesh. The execution of the proper mechanics of the mesh will minimize turnovers. An imaginary clock is used to teach the proper steps for the quarterback. The point where the quarterback takes the exchange from the center is twelve o'clock. The quarterback's stance is balanced, with his feet shoulder width apart and under his armpits. If the inside veer or triple option is being run to the right, then the quarterback will step to three o'clock with his toes pointed to the sideline. If the inside veer or triple option is being run to the left, then the quarterback will step to nine o'clock with his toes pointed to the sideline. The quarterback brings the ball through his playside hip and at the same time extends his arms to mesh with the B-back. The B-back steps with his playside foot at the inside leg of the playside guard from a balanced three-point stance. The quarterback immediately focuses his eyes on the read (the defender upon whom the decision to give or keep will be based) after he takes the snap from the center. The quarterback will read the head and near shoulder of the first down lineman in the B-gap to the outside. The basic rule of thumb for the quarterback is to think give and, if he misses the read, to follow the B-back up in the hole. This read will be an instantaneous read for a quarterback who has the ability to make defenders miss tackles.

The decision to give or keep has to be made by the time the ball reaches the quarterback's front foot. The second step by the quarterback should be no more than two inches wider than his left shoulder (for a right-handed quarterback). There should not be a lot of weight transfer to the front foot, and the quarterback should be able to drop down into a sprinter's stance after riding the B-back. As the quarterback reads the first down lineman from the playside B-gap to the outside, the B-back will read the first down lineman inside the quarterback's read. The B-back should never attempt to cutback during the quarterback's ride. He should keep his shoulders square to the line of scrimmage and read his key. Only after the ball crosses the quarterback's front foot and still remains in his stomach can the B-back grasp it firmly and run to daylight. This concept gives the triple-option attack a chance to run the inside veer and the zone dive at the same time, creating a horizontal stretch.

Ball security is always the major concern in the execution of a proper mesh between the quarterback and the B-back. The B-back should be taught to treat the ball like a bird. If he squeezes it too tightly, it will smother; if he does not squeeze it tightly enough, it will fly away. When the quarterback gives the ball, he should relax his hands. The decision to give or keep can be made no later than when the ball reaches the quarterback's front foot, or the ball may end up on the ground. Once again, repetition is the key to the quarterback and B-back becoming familiar with the feel of the mesh.

The Read Key
There are basically six different types of reads a defensive lineman can give a quarterback. A triple-option quarterback must be able to master all six and be 90 percent proficient at reading them for the first phase of the triple-option attack to be successful. If the quarterback masters five of six reads, the read he sees the majority of the time will be the one he has not yet mastered. Young quarterbacks should be put in read situations in which they can be successful until they master all six different reads. The six reads are as follows:

1. C-stunt (take dive)
2. Squeeze (pad under pad)
3. Mesh Charge (fullback hip to quarterback)
4. Squat (take dive and quarterback)
5. Down the Line (hands squeeze for dive)
6. Cross Charge

Diagram 3-2 illustrates some of the defensive charges described below.

Diagram 3-2

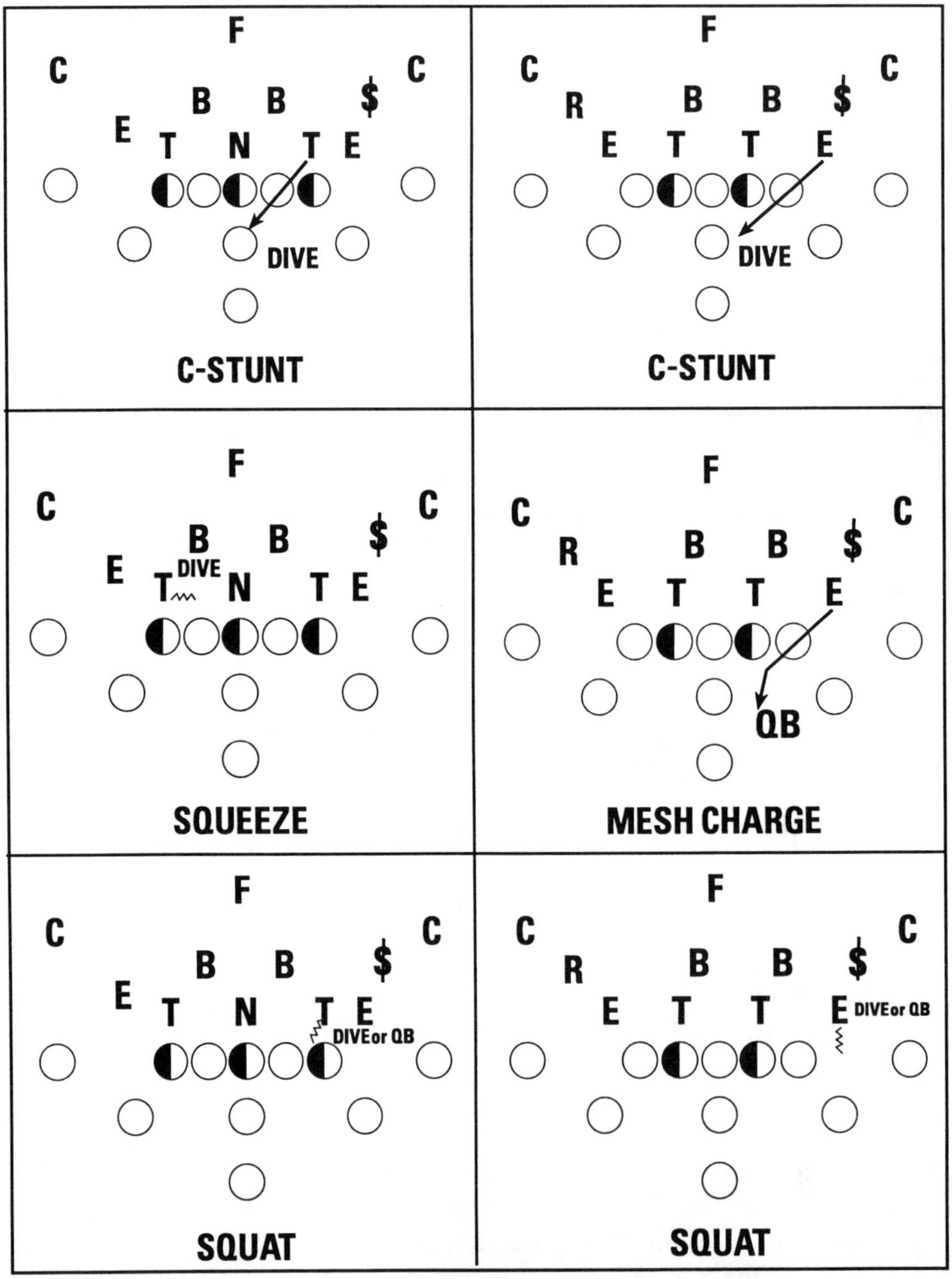

C-STUNT

C-STUNT

SQUEEZE

MESH CHARGE

SQUAT

SQUAT

Diagram 3-2 Cont.

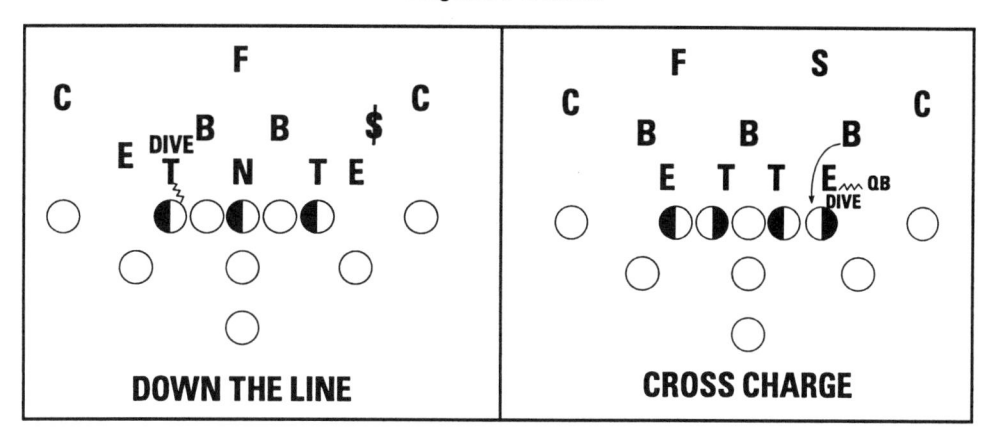

DOWN THE LINE | **CROSS CHARGE**

1. A C-stunt is when a defensive lineman aligned in the B-gap in a 4i or 4 technique makes a distinct, deliberate move without hesitation to tackle the B-back. This is the most common read a quarterback will see and is usually the easiest to master.
2. When a defensive lineman aligned in a 5 technique squeezes with his shoulder pads square to the line of scrimmage to tackle the B-back, it is referred to as a squeeze. Since the evolution of the 4-3 defense, this type of read is not as common as it was during the popularity of the 5-2 defense.
3. A mesh charge occurs when a defensive lineman from any alignment appears to be on a C-stunt but at the last second makes a movement up the field to tackle the quarterback. This is usually the most difficult read for a quarterback to master.
4. When a defensive lineman squats and tries to read the quarterback's decision as the quarterback reads him, it is called a squat.
5. A down the line squeeze by a defensive lineman from a 5 technique alignment is more common today verses 4-3 defenses. This read occurs when the 5 technique squeezes with his hands and not his pads to take the B-back.
6. The final read a quarterback has to master is a cross charge. This particular read is sometimes referred to as an area read, and occurs when a defensive lineman steps out from his alignment to take the quarterback and another defender comes in behind or in front of the quarterback's read to take the dive. Young quarterbacks often have difficulty mastering this read until they become more aware of the whole picture because they tend to focus on specifics rather than generalities (the weakness that this creates elsewhere in the defensive alignment).

Different quarterbacks find different reads more and less difficult to master. When a quarterback has difficulty with one of the six reads, additional repetitions are required on that particular read. Once a defensive team discovers a weakness, they will exploit it until the quarterback proves in a game situation that he can handle it.

Acceleration of the Mesh

Whether the quarterback gives the ball or keeps it and continues on to the pitch key, it is imperative that it appear that he is still in possession of the football. The acceleration off the mesh is what makes defenders overcommit or "bite the cheese." This acceleration creates a false impression that the quarterback has kept the football, making defenders disregard their assigned option responsibilities and leading to big offensive plays from the triple-option attack. One of the worst things the quarterback can do is to look back at the B-back after he has given him the ball. Also, as the quarterback accelerates off the mesh, he should attack the inside or near shoulder of the pitch key. When the quarterback reads the first phase of the triple option and accelerates off the mesh downhill to pitch or keep off the pitch key, he has basically eliminated two defenders without having to block either of them.

Numbers, Grass, and Angles

As the quarterback looks over the defense, there are three basic things he should look for. They are numbers, grass, and angles.

Numbers

A quarterback must be able to count the number of defenders to either side of the ball (Diagram 3-3). The first down lineman aligned in the B gap out is #1, the quarterback's read key. The closest defender outside of #1 and/or stacked behind a 5 technique is #2, the quarterback's pitch key. The closest defender from #2 within five yards of the line of scrimmage is #3.

VEER SCHEME

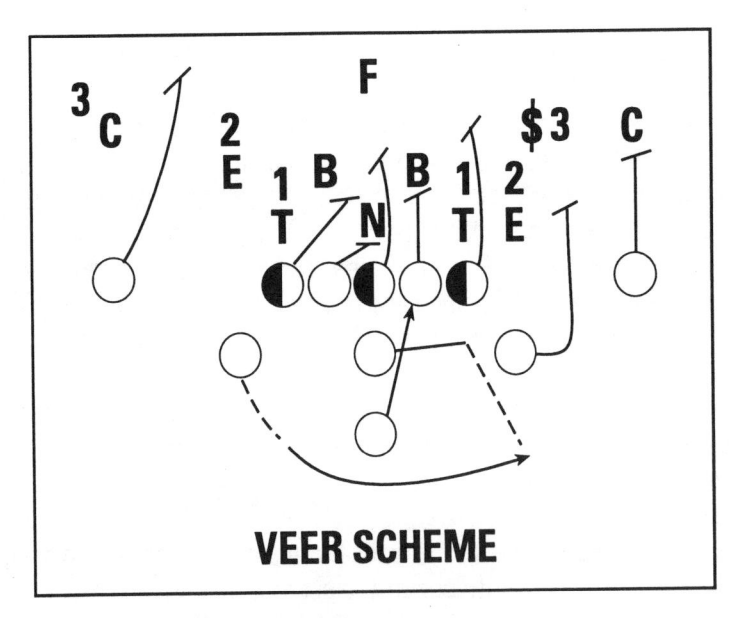

Diagram 3-3

When the quarterback counts to two or less on one side, there is a numbers advantage to that side that has been created by the defensive alignment and should be exploited (Diagram 3-4). If there is a three count to both sides (a balanced defense), the offensive line will use a veer scheme because the playside A-back will have to arc and block run support to the play side. When the quarterback checks the triple option to a two-count side, he will then audible and change the offensive line to a veer-in blocking scheme and the playside A-back will block the linebacker to the safety. His responsibility is called "load path linebacker to safety" and will be explained later in this chapter.

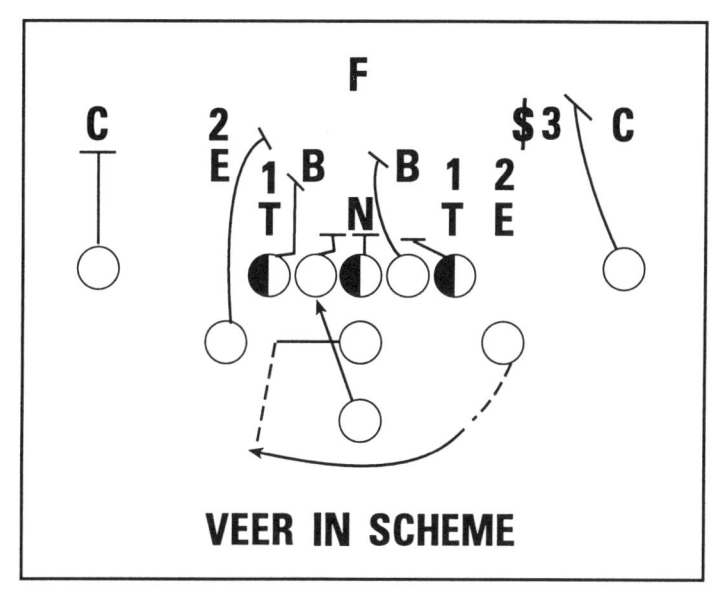

VEER IN SCHEME

Diagram 3-4

Grass
If the quarterback sees that both sides of the ball have a three count, he then looks for the most grass (the wide side of the field). When the ball is in the middle of the field and there is a three count to both sides, then the quarterback will take the play to the call side. If the ball is on the left hash and the count is equal to both sides, the quarterback will take the play to the field. The quarterback will always run the triple option to a two count side, but if the defense has a three count to both sides, then he looks for the most grass and runs the triple option in that direction.

Angles
The last thought process for the quarterback involves the blocking angles for the offensive lineman, A-backs, or wide receivers. If, for example, numbers and grass are equal to both sides but the right offensive tackle's linebacker is aligned wider than the left tackle's linebacker, it is more advantageous to run the triple option to the left (Diagram 3-5). If run support to the right side is aligned at six yards and run

support to the left side is aligned at three yards, there is a better blocking angle for the A-back on the right side, and this is the most advantageous direction to run the triple option. A quarterback can recognize and take advantage of these blocking angles when he has learned the "tricks of the trade" of executing a triple-option attack. Young quarterbacks will have difficulty early in their careers checking the triple option to the most advantageous side of the ball. With practice, they will become adept at making these instantaneous reads. If they do not, then the coach should be training another quarterback who can make the right decision quickly without putting the ball on the ground.

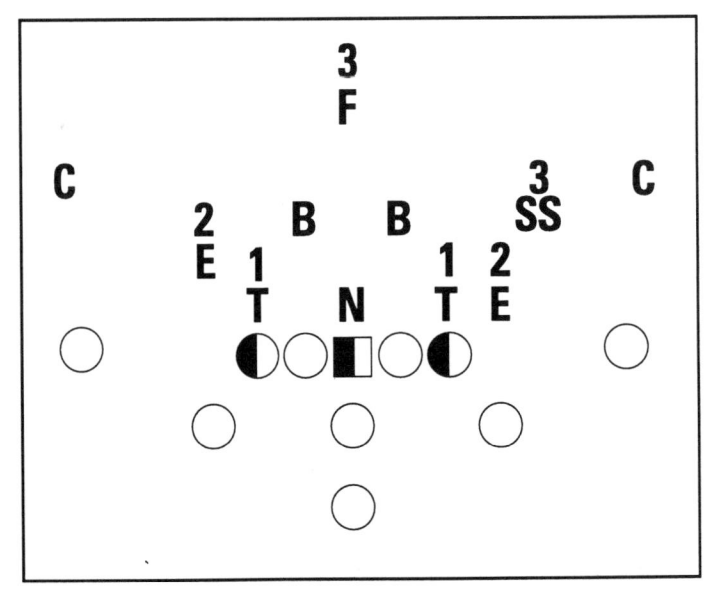

Diagram 3-5

Blocking Techniques
The Offensive Line
A team must have skilled personnel in order to make things happen in the Spread offense, but the offensive linemen are the workhorses that give the offense its power. They have their own special language of communication and are the unsung heroes of the Spread attack. Their most important job is to come off the ball as one and establish a new line of scrimmage on every running play. They should have a tremendous amount of pride when the B-back averages more than five yards per carry. That sort of consistency by the B-back complements the other two phases of the triple option (the keep and the pitch) and makes them much more effective.

There are two basic schemes that the offensive line has to master for the triple option to be properly executed. The first is a loop or veer scheme, which is run to the three-count side and requires the playside A-back to arc block the #3 defender. This play is the base play off the triple option that is most often called in the huddle. 90 percent of the time it is run in the same direction called in the huddle (Diagram 3-3).

The second scheme is an inside scheme or veer-in scheme which is run to a two-count side and requires the playside A-back to block the first inside linebacker not in the count. The veer-in scheme is also referred to as a load scheme, and the A-back's block referred to as a load block (Diagram 3-4).

The Veer Scheme
The basic rule for the playside guard and tackle on the triple option call is veer (Diagrams 3-3 and 3-6). To the playside guard, veer means base. He will block inside, over, outside, or nearest linebacker on a base blocking responsibility. In other words, the playside guard looks for a 2i, 2, or 3 technique defender first; then, if he is uncovered, he will base block the nearest linebacker. The basic rule for the playside tackle is to release outside any down lineman over him, to block the first linebacker over him to the inside, or to release inside when the playside guard is covered by a down lineman. If the playside guard is covered by a down lineman, then the playside tackle will release inside to block the first linebacker over him or to the inside.

VEER SCHEME

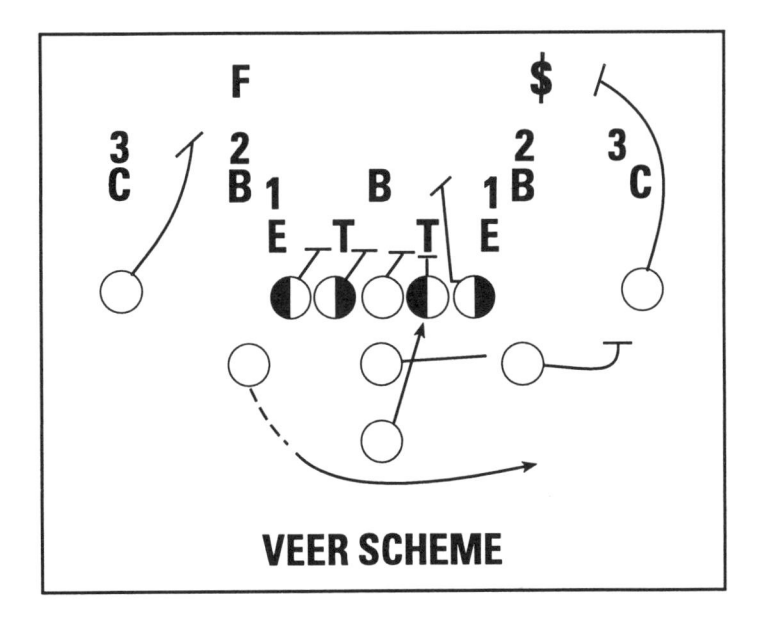

Diagram 3-6

The Scoop
The basic rule for the center and the backside guard and tackle on the veer scheme is to scoop (Diagrams 3-3, 3-4, 3-6, and 3-7). While the playside guard and tackle are blocking veer as described above, the center, backside guard, and backside tackle seal the playside gap to the backside linebacker. They can not allow penetration to interfere with the mesh. The scoop block is pure zone blocking; the center, backside guard, and tackle do not know for sure who they are going to block until after the ball is snapped. The scoop block is not a cut-off block, but rather a read after the first 1.5 steps are taken.

The backside guard and tackle will step at a 45-degree angle toward the playside and then take the first defender who shows up between them and the offensive lineman to the inside. There are times when the angle will have to be less than 45 degrees, especially if the defender is trying to penetrate the gap between him and the next offensive lineman to the inside. If no defender appears after the backside guard or tackle's first 1.5 steps, they will continue on to cut off the backside linebacker.

The center has two types of scoop blocks. If he is uncovered, he runs a wide scoop to seal the playside gap. If he is covered, he runs a tight scoop so the nose can not come out the backside A-gap and disrupt the mesh. The center should reach a shade or 1 technique noseguard and keep him from penetrating the playside A-gap and possibly disturbing the mesh. The B-back will help the center's block in either the tight or wide scoop. If the noseguard's helmet is further to the playside than the center's, the B-back will square his shoulders and run behind the noseguard.

The Veer-In Scheme
The veer-in scheme, sometimes referred to as the load or inside scheme, is employed when the quarterback checks to a two-count side (Diagrams 3-4 and 3-7). This blocking scheme applies to the playside guard and tackle. The center, backside guard, and tackle will scoop block as described above. The playside guard will base block if he is covered and double team the noseguard with the center if he is uncovered. If the playside guard is covered by a down lineman, his base block is as described above (he takes the 2, 2i, or 3 technique defender). If uncovered, the playside guard will call "Ace," which lets the center know to base block and to expect a double-team block from the guard. If the noseguard disappears into the backside A-gap, the playside guard will block the backside linebacker.

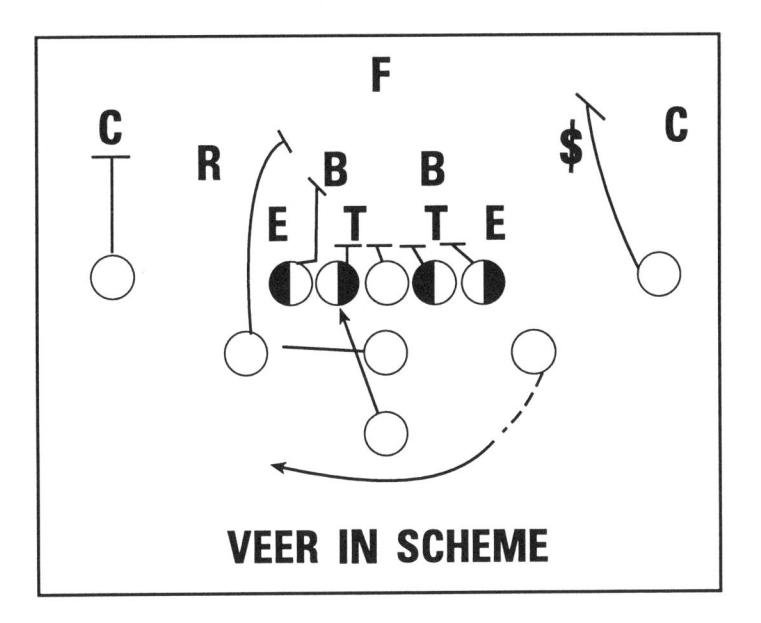

Diagram 3-7

The playside tackle releases inside any down linemen over him to block the first linebacker over him to the inside. He will use an escape technique, stepping with his inside foot up the field and dipping his outside shoulder, attempting to avoid as much contact as possible with any defense linemen over him. Once again, this is the quarterback's read; the playside tackle should escape without contact if possible. He will then continue up field to block the first linebacker over him to the inside.

The Wides
The wide receivers, or wides X and Z (Diagram 2-1), will assume a two-point stance and align near the field numbers. The basic rule for the playside wide is to block run support on a triple option to his side of the field. This will usually mean that he will block a deep third corner in a three-deep scheme or a half-field safety in a two-deep scheme. If load is run to his side, then his basic rule is to block the corner straight up. The backside wideout's rule is to take the best angle and cut off the backside corner. While these positions have the simplest blocking rules to learn, they are not the easiest to execute.

The A-Backs
The playside A-back has two basic rules. If the play is called to his side, he arc blocks #3. If the quarterback checks to his side due to a two count, he load blocks through the playside linebacker not in the count to the safety.

The Arc block is the most difficult for an A-back to master. From his two-point stance with his inside foot back, the playside A-back should step with his playside foot to the sideline on the snap of the ball. He should continue to stay on a flat course with his eyes on #3 for three steps. The most important thing the A-back should do is maintain outside leverage on #3. He continues on his arc path until he gains outside leverage on #3, then accelerates and throws his inside shoulder three inches above #3's outside knee. He should keep his head up and not throw his block until he is close enough to step on #3's foot. If outside leverage can not be achieved, the A-back should stay above the waist and kick #3 to the outside. If outside leverage is accomplished with an effective Arc block, the backside A-back will be further removed from pursuit, creating a better opportunity for a big play. If the playside A-back has to kick out #3, then the backside A-back will have to cut up inside and be closer to the pursuit.

The load block will become the A-back's concern when the quarterback checks the play to his side of the field. If the quarterback spots a numbers advantage that must be exploited, he will check load to that side of the field. The playside A-back will head directly upfield, looking first for the playside linebacker not in the count. If the linebacker is moving in the direction of the play, the A-back will block him to the inside of the field. If the linebacker is "frozen" by the fullback-quarterback fake, or is moving in the wrong direction (away from the play), the A-back will continue upfield and block the free safety (Diagram 3-4).

Once the triple option reads and blocking schemes described above have been mastered, a team can move on to other possibilities created by the Spread. However, the players should remember that these techniques are the bread and butter of the Spread attack. The techniques must be taught, retaught and continually reinforced for all portions of the spread offense to work effectively.

CHAPTER 4

The Zone Dive

The zone dive, or inside zone play, is intended to stretch the playside, cut off the backside and create a vertical seam in which the B-back can run. This play is also good for varying the snap count and keeping the defensive front on its heels. There is also a direct carryover from the teaching of the triple option, especially for the B-back and the offensive line. Since the Spread offense has no plays such as the isolation play or toss sweep, the zone dive is the offense's hard running play. In order for the Spread offense to be effective, the B-back has to get positive yardage on both the give off the triple option, and the predetermined give off the zone dive.

Quarterback
The quarterback's main job on the zone dive is to secure the snap from center and step to five o'clock to the playside, giving the football to the B-back as deep as possible. This allows the B-back a better opportunity to make his reads and square his shoulders sooner than on the triple option. The quarterback can run the zone dive to the call side without having to worry about checking the play. This play is designed to be run regardless of the defensive alignment. After the quarterback gives the football to the B-back, he must do a good job of carrying out his option fake by accelerating from the hand-off and not looking back at the ball carrier. These actions increase the chances of the defenders "biting the cheese," thus creating big play possibilities.

B-Back
The B-back sets up in his three-point stance and steps with his playside foot at the inside leg of the playside guard. His read is the same as on the triple option, the first down lineman inside the quarterback's imaginary read. The quarterback's read is imaginary because the play is a predetermined give to the B-back. The B-back's heels should be 4.5 to 5 yards from the front tip of the ball. This is a quick-hitting play; therefore, the B-back's depth may need to be adjusted if he is not hitting the hole quickly enough. The same principle can be applied to the triple option except that the B-back can square his shoulders sooner running the zone dive because it is a predetermined hand-off and the quarterback is getting him the ball as deep as possible. The first down lineman in the B-gap out is the quarterback's imaginary read, and the B-back's read is the first down lineman inside the quarterback's imaginary read. After the B-back has received the hand-off he should always cover both points of the football as long as he is running inside the tackle box and is no deeper than linebacker depth.

The B-back is basically reading the helmet of the first lineman or linebacker inside the B gap. If his read is the 3 technique, then he will square his shoulders only if the 3 technique's helmet is outside the helmet of the playside guard who is blocking him (Diagram 4-1). If the B-back's read is the shade or 1 technique, then he will square his shoulders only if the shade or 1 technique's helmet is outside the helmet of the center who is trying to reach him (Diagram 4-2). If his read is a 2i technique and the 2i technique's helmet stays inside the guard's helmet, he will continue on his track, watching for a scraping linebacker. If he feels a scraping linebacker, he will square his shoulders at the second level, trying to make the linebacker arm tackle him or over-scrape (Diagram 4-4). There can be no "dancing in the hole." The B-back should make his decision and not look back. The more practice he has reading his keys, the more proficient he will be at running to daylight on the zone dive.

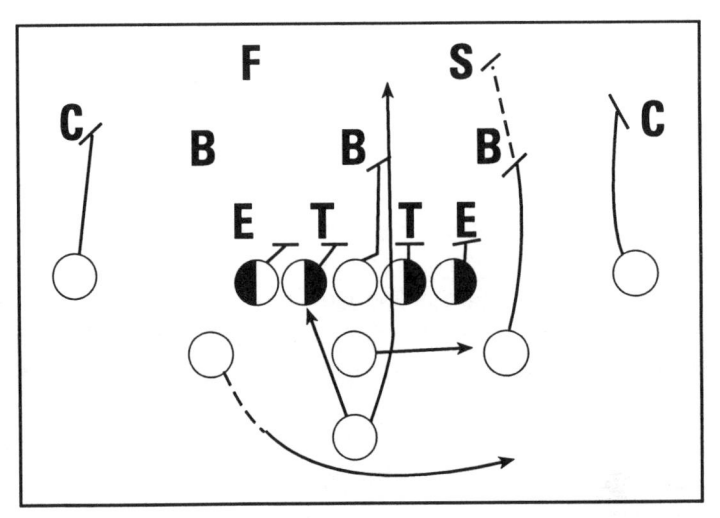

Diagram 4-1

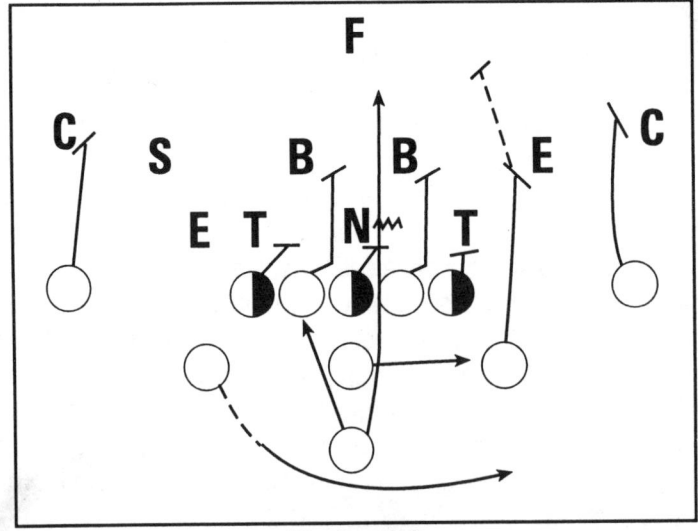

Diagram 4-2

A-Backs

When the zone dive is run on first sound, the backside A-back does not go in tail motion (Diagram 4-3). He will release straight up the field to block any threatening fold player to the safety. The playside A-back also releases straight up the field to block any threatening fold player to the safety. In order to have big plays on the zone dive, the A-backs have to get upfield to block the safeties after they have first checked for any threatening fold players to their side.

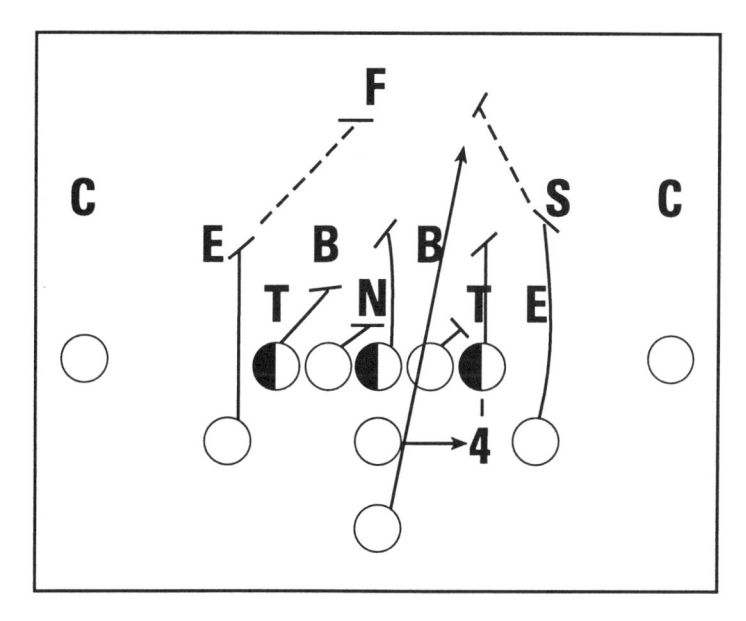

Diagram 4-3

The backside A-back will go in tail motion when the zone dive is run on the normal snap count. This gives the defense a false key and makes defenders stay at home playing option responsibility even though a predetermined give to the B-back is being run.

Wideouts

The rules for X and Z are very simple. They block the man over them inside out. If they are going to lose him, they should lose him to the outside, not to the inside where the ball is being handed off. If the defender over the wideout goes to the outside on the snap of the ball, the wideout can continue on downfield to block the near safety. In this situation the wideouts can cheat further to the outside on their split so the defenders over them are further removed to the outside before the ball is snapped.

Offensive Line Techniques

The offensive line should take pride in running the zone dive because the burden of execution falls on their shoulders. This is an opportunity for the offensive line to have a chance to dominate the line of scrimmage by coming off the ball in unison or in a wave. There are many similarities between the blocking schemes employed with the triple option and the scheme used with the zone dive.

T-Stay

The playside guard and tackle's assignment is called T-stay. "T" means zone, and "stay" means the center has to handle a 1 technique or shade by himself and cannot call for a double team (Ace) with the playside guard. The playside guard and tackle will identify all 2, 2i, 4, and 4i techniques. They take a six-inch zone step with their playside foot to the instep of the first down lineman over them to the outside. They will make their reads as they come off the ball on their first 1.5 steps. If no defender stays in their area after the first 1.5 steps, they turn up the field to block the nearest playside linebacker (Diagram 4-3).

If the playside guard and tackle are both covered by down linemen, the playside tackle will make a "base" call. This alerts the playside guard to the fact that the tackle also has a man over him, and therefore the guard should zone step to the first down lineman over him to the outside (Diagram 4-4).

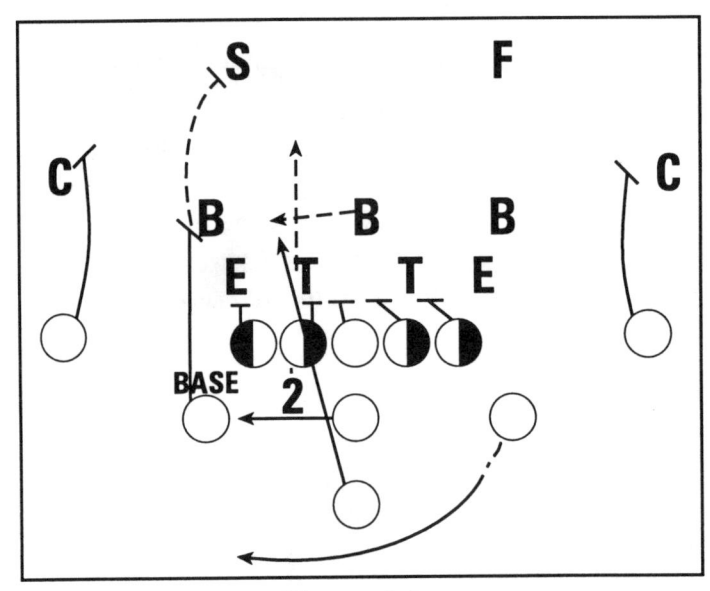

Diagram 4-4

Scoop

The same scoop blocking technique used with the veer or veer-in scheme is used with the T-stay scheme while blocking for zone dive play. The offensive line should prevent penetration into the backfield where the hand-off is taking place.

CHAPTER 5

The Trap

The trap play was originally intended to complement the trap option. The trap option was designed to be the more dominant play because most defenses were five-man fronts or 50 defenses and most 5 technique defensive tackles were readers, not penetrators as they are today with the attacking style 4-3 defenses. Most 5 techniques would squeeze versus a veer-in scheme or inside blocking scheme, making it easier for a pulling guard to log, or block to the inside, a 5 technique with the backside guard and take the ball outside. The trap has recently become more popular because defensive fronts are attacking the line of scrimmage on the snap of the ball and getting up the field. This creates a better opportunity to trap, especially against 2, 2i, and 3 technique defenders who are penetrating up the field. An attacking style 4-3 defense also presents less opportunity to log a 5 technique defender inside and run outside. Another plan was to not let the 5 technique know whether he was going to be trapped or logged by the backside pulling guard. With the widespread usage of the attacking style 4-3, which usually covers both offensive guards, it has become much more difficult to execute this diversion because the playside guard has to hold his block too long. Therefore the focus of whom to trap is now directed at the 2, 2i, and 3 techniques.

Quarterback
The quarterback's basic rule of thumb is to run the play to the widest inside technique. For example, if a shade or 1 technique is the widest technique on the right and there is a 3 technique on the left, then the quarterback would run the play to the 3 technique side (Diagram 5-1). The quarterback will reverse pivot by taking two six o'clock steps. If the play is being run to the right, the quarterback will take his first six o'clock step with his left foot, opening up away from the playside and making a positive exchange with the B-back. His second six o'clock step will be with his right foot. At this point the quarterback will carry out his trap-option fake down the line of scrimmage. It is just as important for the quarterback to accelerate from the mesh without the ball as is for him to follow through when he has the ball. This action increases the likelihood that the defenders will "bite the cheese" or lose sight of the ball.

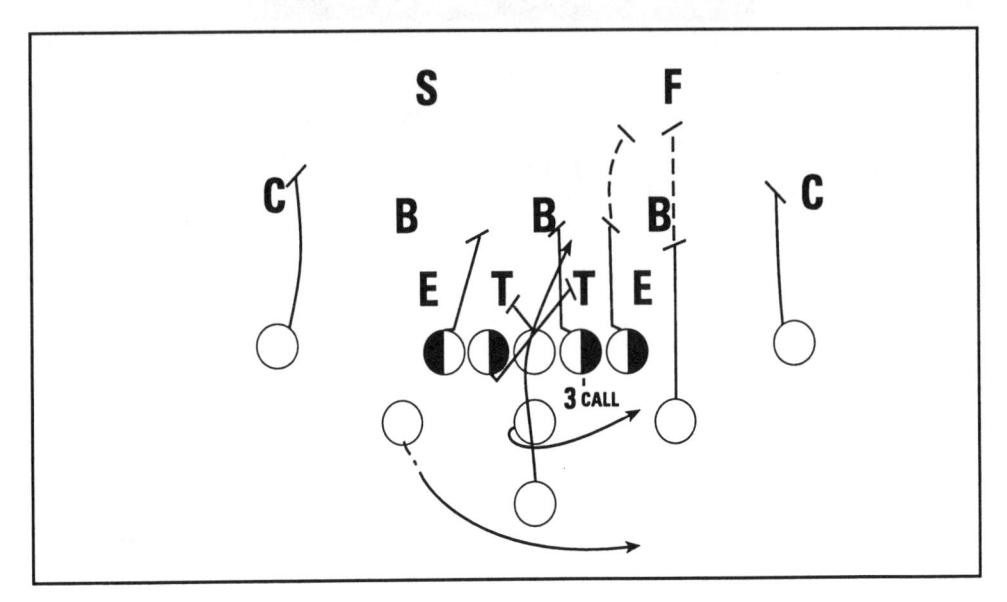

Diagram 5-1

B-Back
The B-back starts from his three-point stance, steps with his playside foot to the backside of the center, and takes the hand-off. The B-back will follow the pulling guard's hip until he sees daylight. He then becomes a north and south runner. Once again, it is extremely important that, after receiving the hand-off, he covers both points of the football while he is running in the tackle box and is no deeper than linebacker depth.

A-Backs
The playside A-back's rule is to release straight up the field to block any threatening fold player to safety. The backside A-back will go in tail motion prior to the snap of the ball and continue through the heels of the B-back on his pitch path. Tail motion, along with the quarterback carrying out the option fake, helps keep defenders at home playing their option responsibility. Similar to the zone dive, the playside A-back needs to get down field to block the safety after he has first checked for any threatening fold player to his side. If the B-back breaks clean into the secondary, the safeties are one of the few remaining obstacles. A good A-back will get out in front of the runner and throw some downfield blocks on the safeties.

Wides
The rules for X and Z are the same on the trap play as the zone dive. The wideout should block the man over him inside out. If he is going to lose him, he should lose him to the outside, not to the inside where the ball is being handed off. As on the zone dive, X and Z can cheat their splits further to the outside so the defenders over them are farther away from the hand-off.

Offensive Line

There are basically two kinds of traps, long traps or short traps. The long trap is when the backside pulling guard traps the first down lineman in the B gap out (Diagrams 5-2 and 5-3). A short trap, also known as a quick trap, is when the backside pulling guard traps the 1st down lineman in the playside A-gap to the outside (Diagrams 5-1 and 5-4).

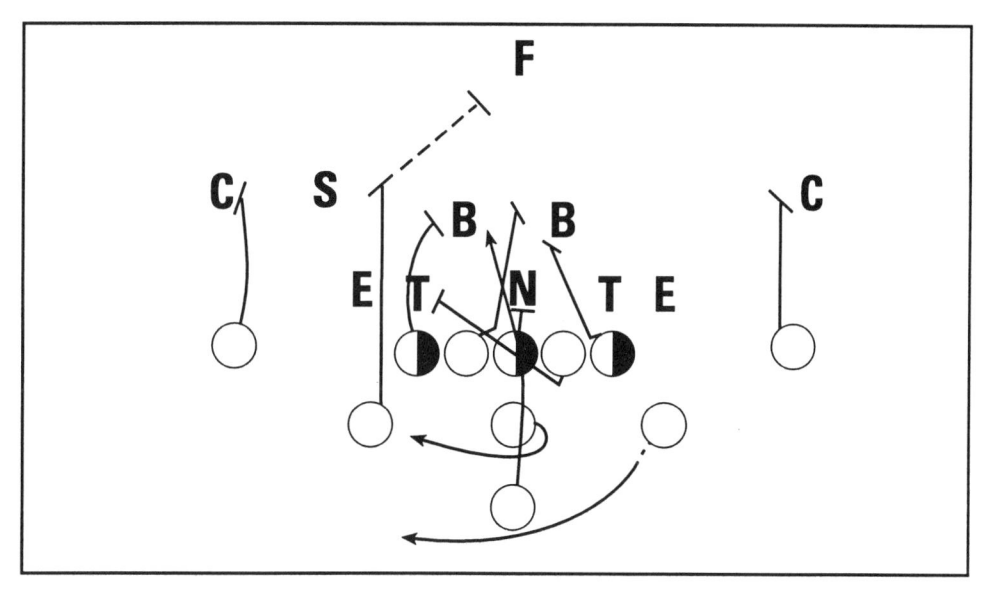

Diagram 5-2

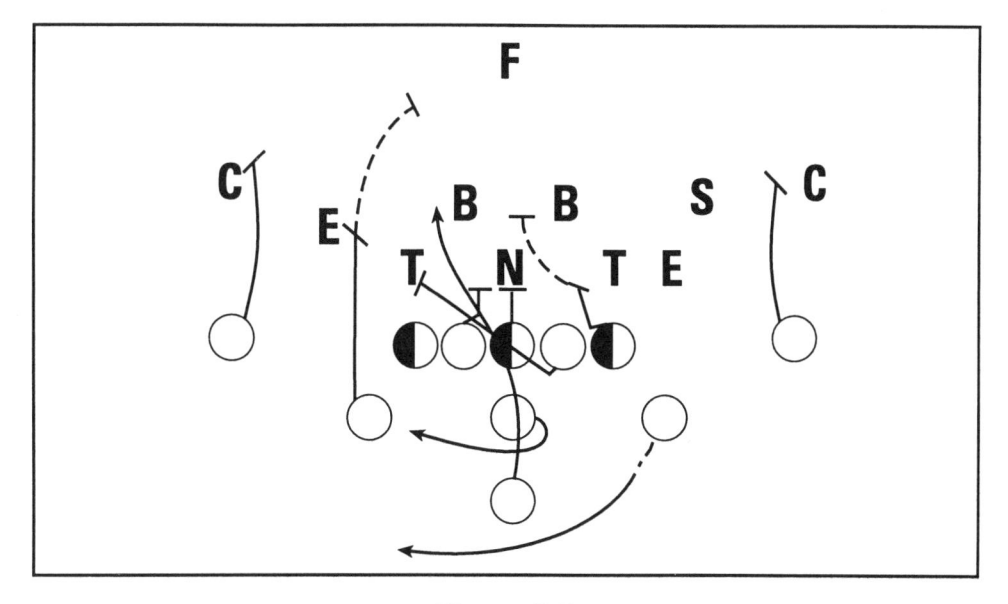

Diagram 5-3

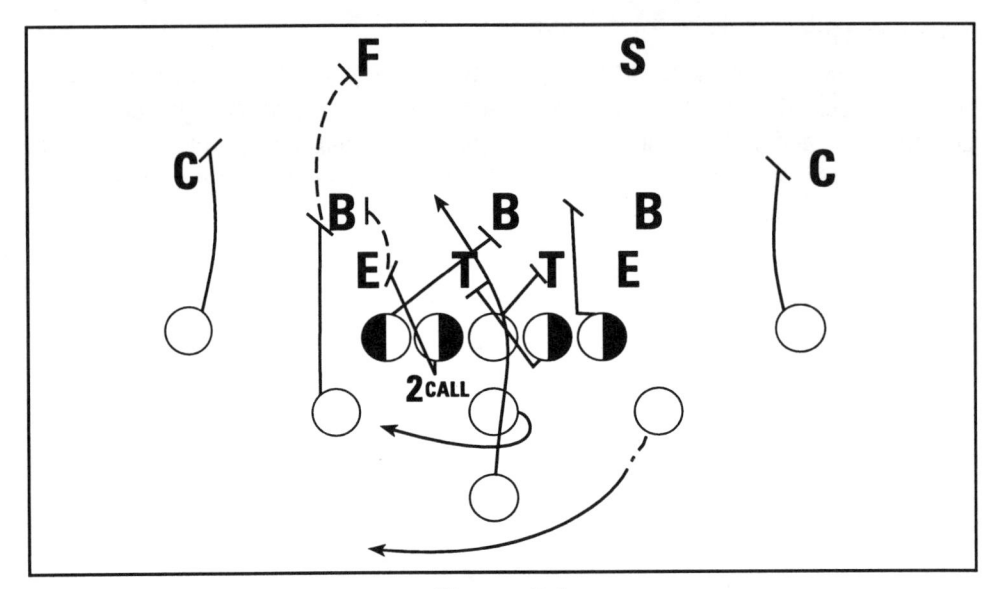

Diagram 5-4

The quick trap is very effective versus the 4-3 penetrating defenses.

Long traps are generally more effective versus 5-2 or 50 defenses. This is especially true when the trap option is included in the package because of the added pressure on the 5 technique of not knowing whether the pulling guard is trying to trap him to the outside or log him to the inside.

Veer In or Out
The basic blocking scheme for the playside guard and tackle is veer in or out. This scheme is setup for the long trap first, which will automatically convert to a quick trap when there is an A gap, 2, 2i, or 3 technique. The playside tackle's rule is to release inside or outside any down lineman over him to block the first linebacker over him to the inside (Diagrams 5-2 and 5-3). A two or three call by the playside guard calls off this long trap and converts it to a short trap (Diagrams 5-1 and 5-4). A three call tells the playside tackle to release inside any down lineman over him to block any B gap linebacker to threatening fold player to safety. A two call tells the playside tackle to release through the hip of the 2 technique to block the first linebacker over the center to the playside. It is imperative that the playside tackle take the proper angle to have the best chance to block the linebacker. If he is not flat enough, he will never get to the linebacker.

The playside guard's rule is to two or three call, to Ace, or to railroad track to the backside linebacker. He makes a two or three call if he is covered by a down lineman, he doubles with center against the noseguard (Ace) if he is uncovered, and he railroad tracks to the backside linebacker if the noseguard goes weak. If he has an A gap player (a defensive lineman in the A gap not touching the center or playside guard by alignment), 2, or 2i technique he will make a two call. A two call tells the playside guard to influence (show pass) and block out through the inside shoulder of the down lineman over the playside tackle to any threatening fold player to safety (Diagram 5-4). A three call tells the playside guard to release inside the 3 technique to block the first linebacker over him to the inside (Diagram 5-1).

The center's rule is to block back all the way to a 3 technique. In other words, he is filling for the pulling guard to the backside. The backside guard needs to identify any technique over him so the center will know who he is blocking. If the center does not get a call from the backside, then he will base block the noseguard or 1 technique.

The backside guard's rule is to pull up into the line of scrimmage and trap the first down lineman in the B gap out. The backside guard cannot let the defender being trapped cross his face back to the inside where the B-back is running. If the backside guard gets a two or three call, he will pull up into the line of scrimmage to trap the first down lineman in the A gap out. This will require the backside guard to go up in the line of scrimmage at a sharper angle than when trapping any B gap player to the outside. Once again, it is imperative that the pulling guard not allow the defender being trapped to cross his face or wrong shoulder the trapper and make the B-back bounce the play to the outside.

The backside tackle's rule is to inside release any down lineman over him to cut off the backside linebacker. The backside tackle must take a good angle to cut off the backside linebacker. For example, if the backside guard is uncovered, then the backside tackle should go through the heels of the noseguard to cutoff the backside linebacker.

Whenever the offense starts to become stymied by quick, attacking, and penetrating defensive linemen, the trap can be a very effective and potent offensive weapon.

CHAPTER 6

The Trap Option

The trap option can be run with several different backfield actions, giving defenses different looks with only minimal changes in offensive assignments. This approach adheres to the KISS principle, the basic principle of the Spread offense. Even though it can be more difficult to execute the trap-option scheme versus a 4-3 attacking style defense, it can still be very effective.

One very good complement to the trap option is the triple option. There are times, even versus 4-3 schemes, that during the course of a game the 5 technique will begin to squeeze harder than he initially did at the beginning of the game. This opportunity is a natural progression set up when the offense reads its way from the inside to the outside running the triple option. After having run the inside plays, the 5 technique will be easier to log for the backside guard and the ball can be taken outside on the perimeter via the trap option. The trap option is the spread offense's double option play and a way for a team to take the ball outside without having to read its way out.

There are two different backfield actions that can be used while implementing the trap option. The first is the same action as the trap which makes both plays look the same to opposing defenses (Diagrams 6-1 and 6-2). The second is a counter option which takes advantage of defenses trying to make pre-snap adjustments to tail motion (Diagrams 6-3 and 6-4).

Quarterback
The quarterback uses the same count system for the trap option as he does for the triple option. The triple option requires the quarterback to read #1 and pitch off #2, and the A-back blocks run support or #3. If the quarterback counts to two or less on one side, he can change the scheme to a load scheme which sends the playside A-back to block through the playside linebacker to the safety (Diagram 6-1). With the trap option, the backside guard or playside tackle, however it unfolds, will take care of #1. The quarterback will still pitch off #2 and the A-back still blocks run support or #3. As with the triple option, if the quarterback counts to two or less on one side, he can change the scheme to a load scheme which sends the playside A-back to block linebacker to safety.

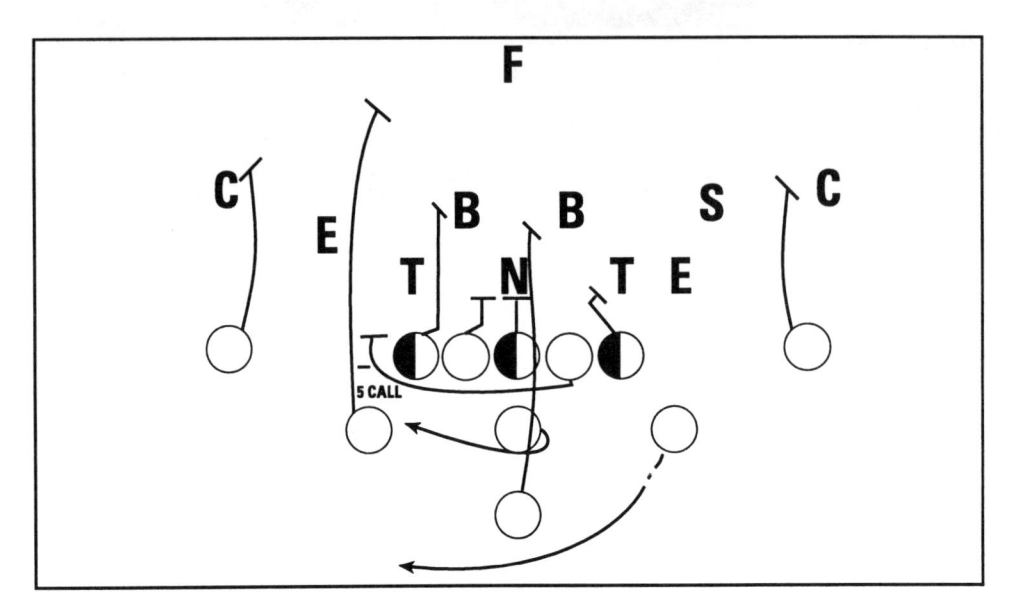

Diagram 6-1

The quarterback's thought process is the same on the trap option as on the triple option: numbers, grass, angles.

On the trap option, the quarterback will use the same steps as on the trap (Diagrams 6-1 and 6-2). He will reverse pivot by taking two six o'clock steps. If the play is being run to the right, then the quarterback will take his first six o'clock step with his left foot opening up away from the playside, making sure he seats the ball to keep the backside guard from knocking it loose. His second six o'clock step will be with his right foot. It is imperative that the quarterback get his head around with his second six o'clock step in order to handle a #2 defender coming hard for the quarterback on the snap of the ball. If #2 is coming hard, the quarterback will pitch the ball to the backside A-back in tail motion. If #2 is not coming hard for the quarterback, he will continue downhill to attack the inside shoulder of #2, forcing him to make a decision whether or not to take the quarterback. It is important for the quarterback to apply pressure to the #2 defender rather than respond to it.

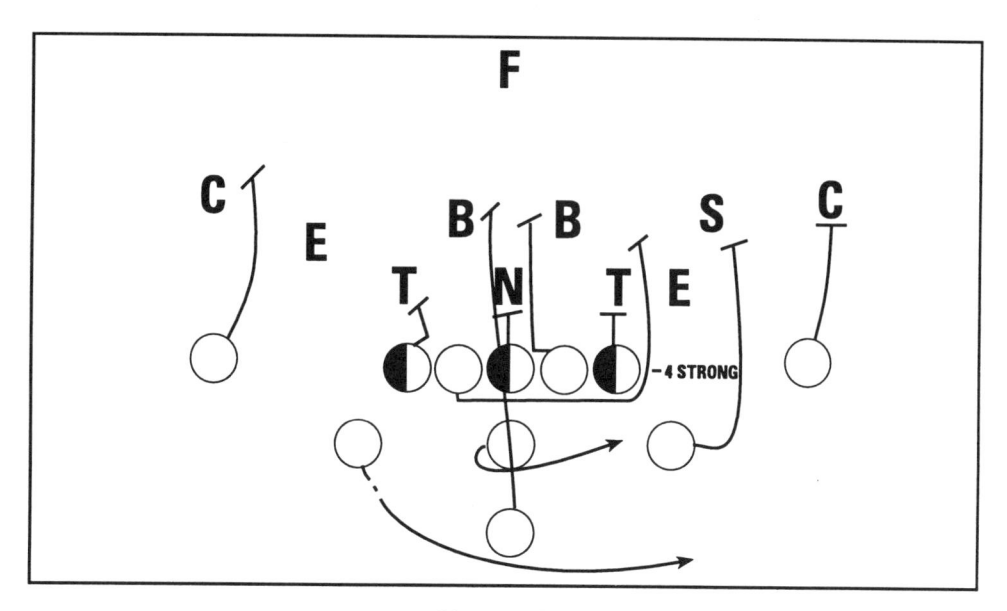

Diagram 6-2

On the counter-trap option play, the quarterback should find a soft #2 to run the play to (Diagrams 6-3 and 6-4). The count system is still the same; however, the counter-trap option is best run to the side where there is not a threat of #2 coming hard at the quarterback on the snap of the ball. If the counter-trap option play is being run to the right, the quarterback will step to three o'clock with his left foot, then reverse pivot back into the line of scrimmage and continue on his option path to attack the inside shoulder of #2. The steps taken by the quarterback on the counter-trap option play do not put him in an advantageous position to handle a #2 coming hard at him on the snap of the ball. The count system remains the same and the quarterback can check to a load scheme (A-back blocks linebacker to safety) if an advantageous two-count side is identified.

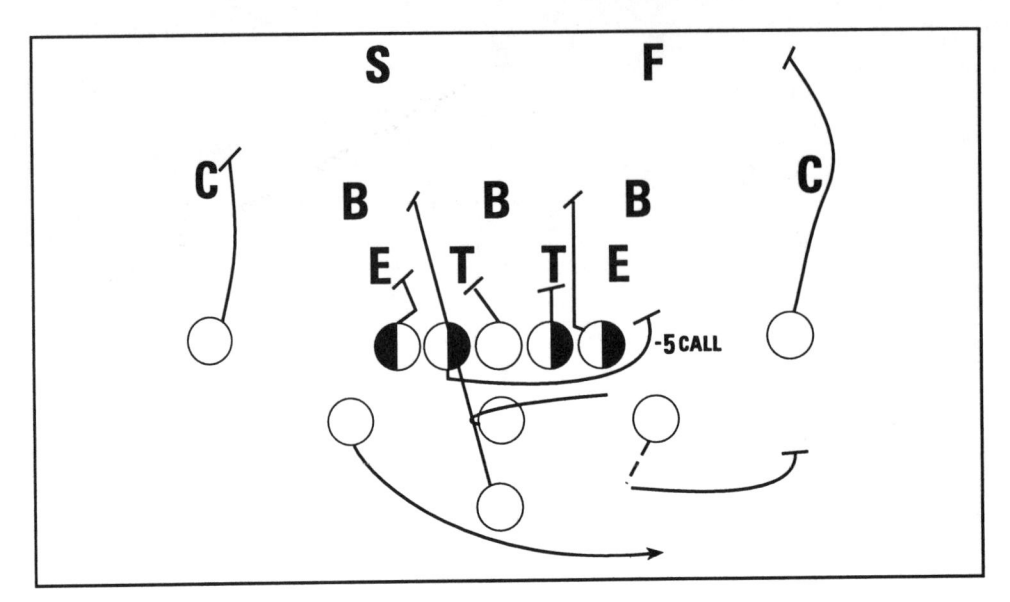

Diagram 6-3

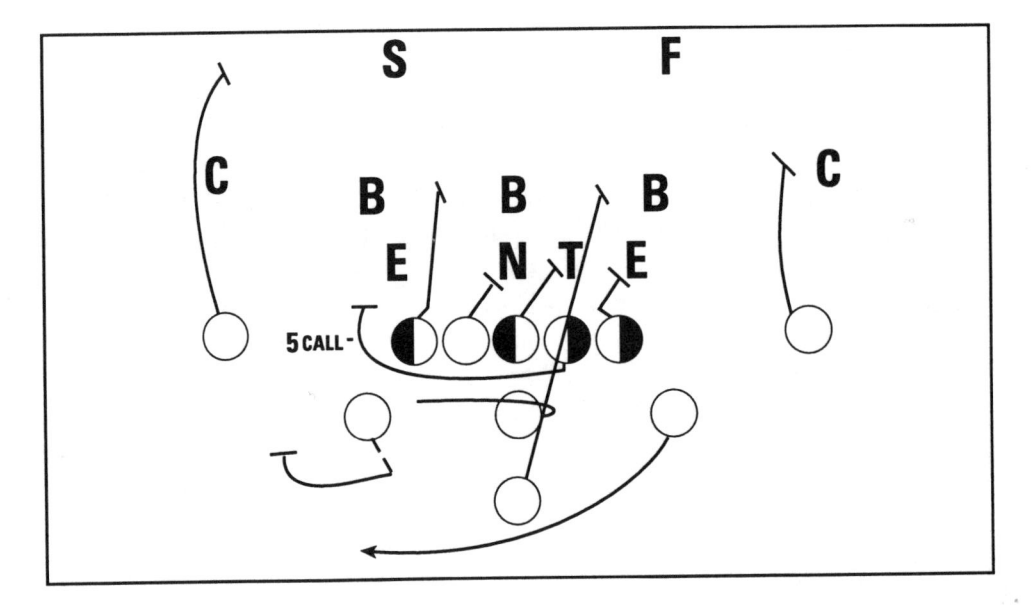

Diagram 6-4

B-Back

The B-back will use the same steps on the trap option as he does on the trap. From his three-point stance, he will step with his playside foot to the backside of the center, faking the trap. He then continues following the guard's hip to block a middle linebacker or run through to the backside linebacker to safety (Diagrams 6-1 and 6-2).

On the counter-trap option, the B-back will step with his backside foot to the inside leg of the backside or pulling guard, faking the triple option with the quarterback, and continue on to block the backside linebacker to safety (Diagrams 6-3 and 6-4).

On the counter-trap option play, the B-back is going at an angle that will not allow him to block a middle linebacker run-through.

A-Backs

On the trap option, the playside A-back will arc block #3 with the same technique he used when blocking the triple option (Diagram 6-2). The backside A-back will go in tail motion prior to the snap of the ball, gaining 1 to 1.5 steps before the ball is snapped, and continue on his pitch path through the heels of the B-back's alignment. The playside A-back on the counter-trap option will go in twirl motion prior to the snap of the ball (Diagrams 6-3 and 6-4). He takes three steps as if he were a backside A-back going in tail motion. On the third step, the playside A-back will open his hips parallel to the line of scrimmage, reversing his direction to the playside. Now the playside A-back will continue on his arc path to block #3. If the quarterback did check to a load scheme prior to the snap of the ball, the playside A-back will go downhill on his third step just off the playside tackle's hip on his load path linebacker to safety. At first it may not appear that twirl motion would have a significant effect on defenders, but it does. Because of the balanced formation and tail motion, defenses are always trying to gain an advantage by getting a jump on tail motion prior to the snap. Twirl motion forces defenses to remain balanced and not overcommit. The backside A-back on the counter-trap option play will not go in tail motion but will start on his pitch path at the snap of the ball. Because of the counter action by the quarterback and B-back, this action will buy time for the backside A-back to get around on his pitch path and stay in pitch relationship with the quarterback.

Wides

The rules for X and Z are the same as on the triple option. The playside wideout's rule on the trap option and counter-trap option is to block run support. This is usually a deep third corner in a three-deep scheme and a half-field safety in a two-deep scheme. If the quarterback checks to a load scheme prior to the snap of the ball, then the wideout's basic rule is to block the corner straight up (Diagram 6-1). The backside wideout's rule is to take the best angle to cut off the backside corner.

Offensive Line

The blocking schemes for the offensive line on both the trap option and the counter-trap option are the same. One of the most difficult things for an offensive lineman to execute in the Spread offense is pulling on the trap option and counter-trap option. Once the backside pulling guard has had an adequate amount of practice pulling and sealing the 5 technique area, these two trap-option schemes can be an integral part of the Spread attack.

Veer-In

The veer-in scheme on the trap option and counter-trap option is very similar to the veer-in scheme on the loaded-triple option. This scheme is the base scheme on both trap-option plays, so if the quarterback checks the play at the line of scrimmage to a load scheme for the playside A-back, the offensive linemen do not have to change their base assignments because the veer-in scheme is already built in. Veer-in applies to the playside tackle and guard. The playside tackle releases inside any down lineman over him to block the first linebacker over him to the inside. He will use the same escape technique that he used on the triple option loaded scheme: he steps with his inside foot up the field, dipping his outside shoulder and trying to avoid contact with any defensive lineman over him. He will continue climbing up the field to block the first linebacker over him to the inside. The playside guard base blocks if he is covered by a down lineman (2, 2i, or 3 technique) and double teams the noseguard with the center by making an Ace call if he is uncovered. If the noseguard or 1 technique disappears to the backside A gap, then the playside guard will continue up the field to block the backside linebacker. The center's rule is to block back all the way to a 3 technique. If there is not a 3, 2, 2i, A gap player, or 1 technique to go back on, then the center will base block the noseguard. If the center has a shade on his playside and a defender to go back on, then the Ace call by the playside guard will be overruled by a down call (Diagram 6-4) by the center. This situation also applies to the trap scheme. The down call by the center tells the playside guard that he must take a good angle in order to handle the 1 technique by himself because the center has to go back on a 3, 2, 2i, A gap player, or 1 technique. If this backside defender is not picked up by the center, he could run the play down from the back, creating havoc in the backfield.

The backside guard will pull and seal the 5 technique area. The playside tackle will make a four or five call (Diagrams 6-1, 6-3, and 6-4) before the ball is snapped to give the backside guard a better idea of what might occur after the ball is snapped. The backside guard will step with his playside foot and pull flat down the line of scrimmage to log the 5 technique's outside leg. If the 5 technique gets too far up the field, the guard will kick him out and the quarterback will go up inside #1 looking for #2 or his pitch key. The playside tackle will treat a head-up 4 technique and a 5 technique the same way by making a five call. The playside tackle will use an escape technique versus both a head-up 4 technique and a 5 technique. If the playside tackle gives a four strong call (versus a 4i technique, Diagram 6-2) prior to the snap of the ball, he will then base block the 4i and the backside guard will turn up off the hip of the playside tackle to block the first inside linebacker not in the count.

It is important that the pulling guard get enough repetitions in practice to become comfortable identifying his assignment and executing his blocks versus the various looks he is going to see come game time. The backside tackle's rule is to anchor down to stack. This means the backside tackle has to take the inside away and pass protect a 4, 4i, 5, 6, or 7 technique. If he has a defender in the backside B-gap, he will have no choice but to scoop the B-gap defender. The stack rule means that as he anchors down, he also needs to peek inside for any possible linebacker run through the backside B-gap. If the backside tackle did not have the anchor down rule, the quarterback could easily be run down from behind because of the counter action in the backfield.

CHAPTER 7

The Speed Option

The theory behind the speed option is very similar to that of the trap option. There is also a tremendous amount of teaching carry-over from the trap option to the speed option. The speed option came about because of the widespread use of the attacking style 4-3 defense. This play is specifically designed to take advantage of a 5 technique defender who will not squeeze inside, and it allows the offense to get the ball pitched and on the perimeter quickly.

Quarterback
The quarterback will employ the same count system with the speed option as with the triple option and trap option. In lieu of the count system, the quarterback should first look for a soft #2 to run the speed option to, and from there apply the general rule of numbers, grass, and angles. On this version of the speed option, the quarterback is looking to pitch the ball off of #1, the playside A-back will block a soft #2, and the B-back will arc run support with the quarterback pitching off #1 to the backside A-back (Diagrams 7-1 and 7-2). If the quarterback does not find a soft #2 to either side, he will check to a load scheme (Diagrams 7-3 and 7-4). The basic reason for the check is because the playside A-back, more often than not, will have a very difficult time trying to block a #2 defender on the line of scrimmage. Therefore, the quarterback will check to a load scheme, which tells the playside A-back to block the playside linebacker to the safety and the backside pulling guard or the playside tackle to block #1.

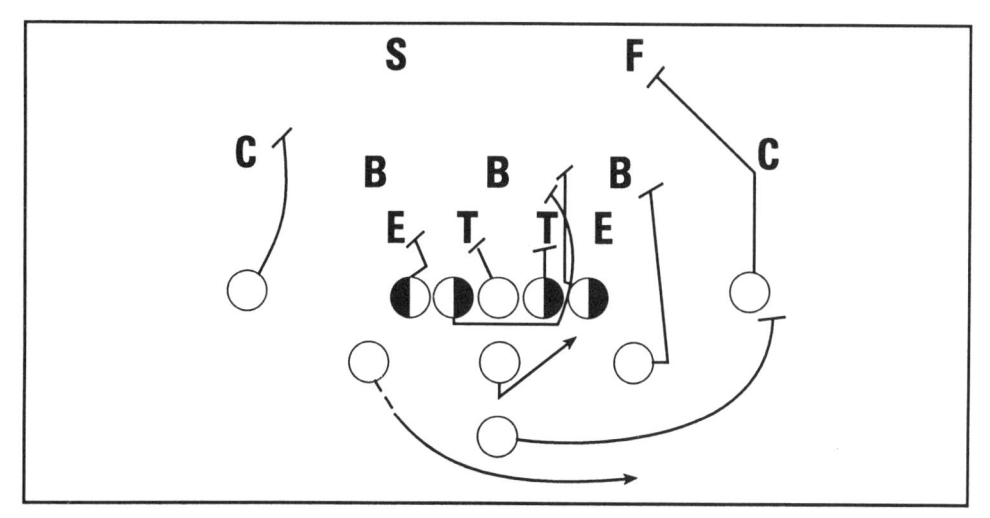

Diagram 7-1

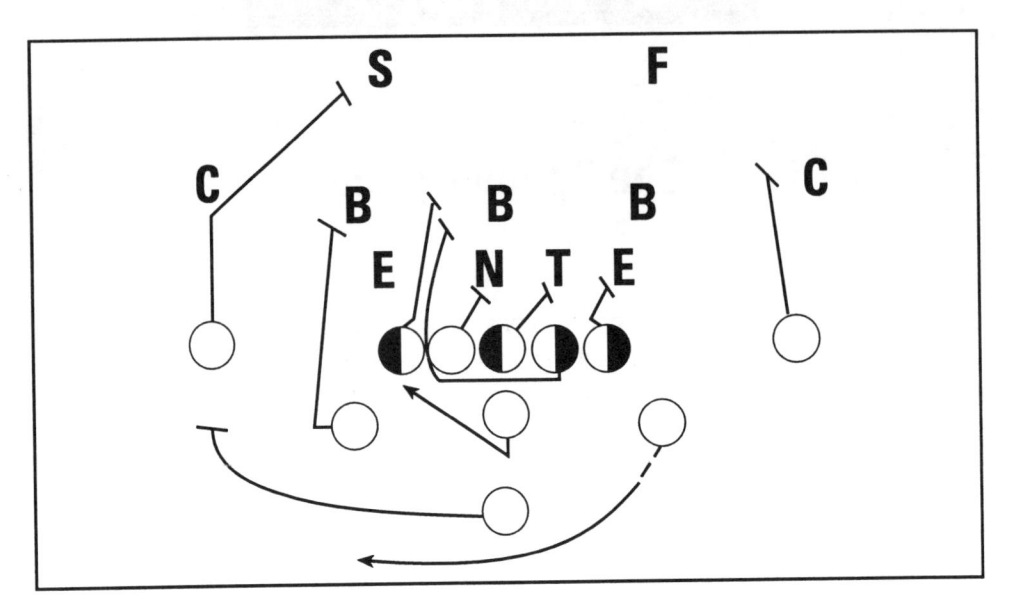

Diagram 7-2

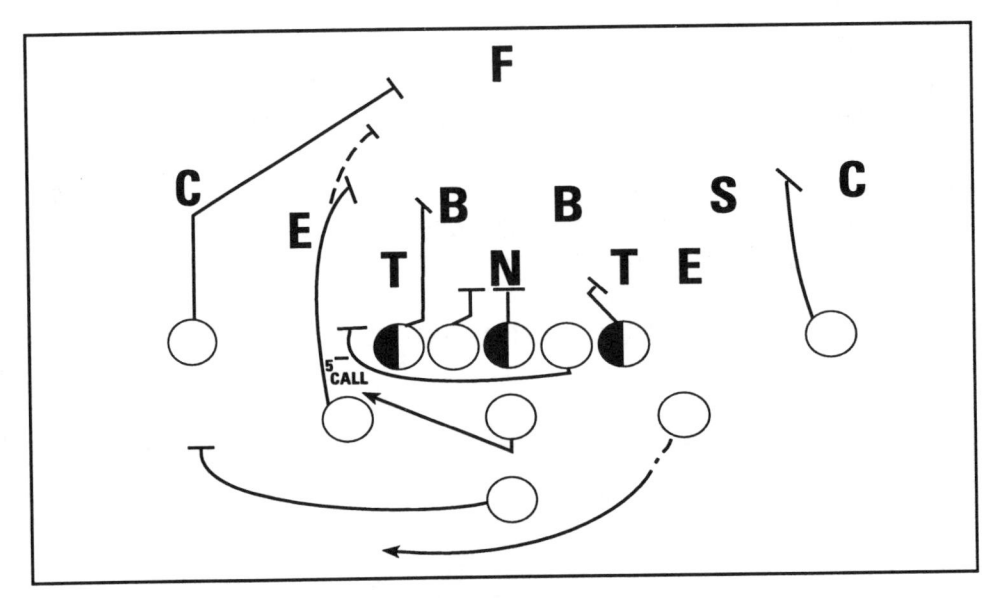

Diagram 7-3

48

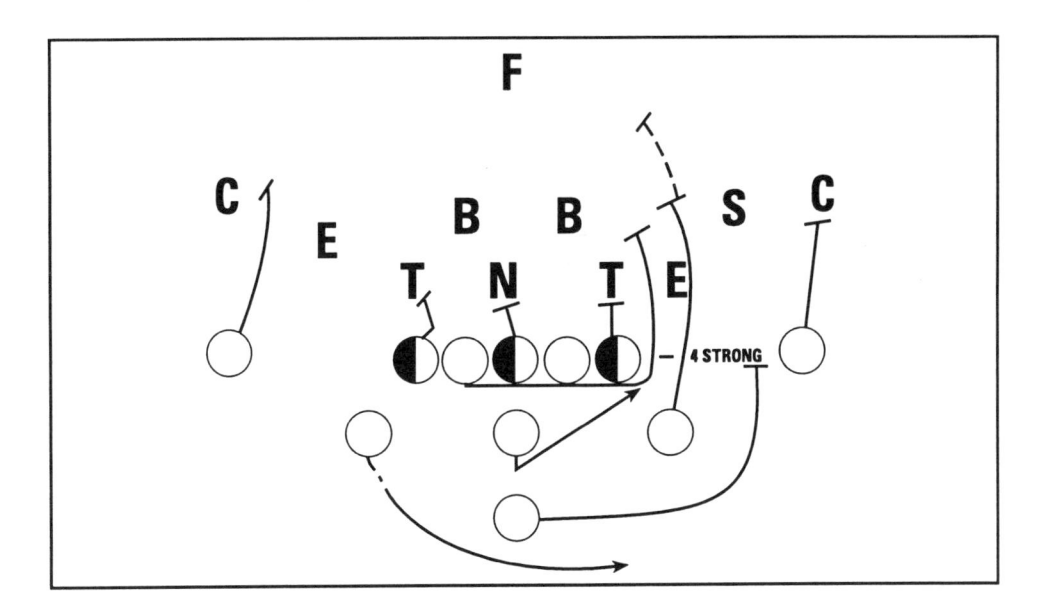

Diagram 7-4

The B-back will still block run support by arc blocking to the playside. Once the quarterback has checked to a trap option with load scheme, the blocking assignments and techniques for the offensive line are the same as those discussed in Chapter Six.

The fundamentals for the quarterback are identical on both versions of the speed option. If the speed option is being run to the right, the quarterback will open pivot, stepping with his right foot to six o'clock. He will gather his left foot and pause, immediately looking to #1. The quarterback should be ready to pitch the ball quickly.

This pitch happens much more quickly than any other option play in the Spread offense. Pitching off #1 allows the ball to get to the corner right away. It is basically a sweep play with option principles, but the playside tackle is not asked to reach a 5 technique. If the quarterback has checked to a load scheme, then he will employ the same steps (the pause is more important with the load scheme because it buys time for the guard to get out in front) but will continue down the line attacking the inside shoulder of #2.

B-Back
The B-back will block run support using the arc technique discussed earlier. He must ensure that outside leverage is maintained or that they are kicked to the outside (safety or corner—this is called ensuring safety to corner). The B-back should learn the count system, but from his alignment it is more difficult for him to recognize where #1, #2, and #3 are located. Therefore, it is simpler for him to arc run support ensuring safety to corner. The B-back will step with his playside foot pointed to the

sideline, continuing on his arc path. His arc path should be flat, drifting no more than two feet closer to the line of scrimmage until he clears the tackle box or the playside tackle's outside foot. The B-back will use the same arc technique that the A-backs use, trying to gain outside leverage on run support. When outside leverage is achieved, the B-back can work upfield, throwing his inside shoulder three inches above the safety or corner's outside knee. He should keep his head up and wait to throw his block until he can step on the defender's foot.

If the defender beats the B-back upfield or crosses his face, the B-back should stay high and kick the safety or corner outside. This is not ideal because the pitch back will have to turn up inside the B-back's kick-out block and will therefore be closer to the pursuit.

A-Backs
The playside A-back's rule on the speed option is to block #2 (Diagrams 7-1 and 7-2). The technique he will use is called a read step. On the snap of the ball the playside A-back will take a flat read step to buy time for the play to develop and to ensure that his block on #2 will occur about the time the ball will be pitched. After he takes his read step, the playside A-back will accelerate upfield to throw his inside shoulder three inches above the outside knee of the #2 defender. A simpler way to define the read step technique is to consider it a slight pause before the A-back accelerates to block #2.

The backside A-back will go in tail motion, gaining 1 to 1.5 steps prior to the snap of the ball while staying on his pitch path. If the quarterback checks to the loaded-speed option, the playside A-back will load block the first inside playside linebacker not in the count because the quarterback will pitch the ball off #2 (Diagrams 7-3 and 7-4). The backside A-back's assignment on the speed option and loaded-speed option is the same tail motion.

Wides
The rules for X and Z are the same on the speed option and loaded-speed option. The playside wideout's rule is to "push crack" unless he has an inverted safety. In that case he would block the corner straight up. When the playside wide "push cracks," he needs to stop the charge of the corner before he releases to block the safety (Diagrams 7-1, 7-2, and 7-3) in order to help maintain a softer corner and set up the B-back's arc block. The backside wideout's rule is to take the best angle to cut off the backside corner.

Offensive Line
The basic blocking scheme for the speed option and the loaded-speed option is veer-in, with only a small adjustment made for the speed option. On the speed option the veer-in scheme used is identical to the trap option veer-in scheme. The playside

tackle releases inside any down lineman over him to block the first linebacker over him to the inside. He uses the same escape technique used on the triple option and trap option.

The playside guard base blocks if he is covered by a down lineman, double teams the noseguard with the center if he is uncovered (Ace), and railroad tracks to the backside linebacker if the noseguard disappears to the backside A gap. The center will block back all the way to a 3 technique. If there is not a 1 technique, A gap defender, 2, 2i, or 3 technique, the center will base block the noseguard. The only change involves the backside guard on the speed option. Since the quarterback is looking to pitch off of #1, the backside guard will pull and turn up to ensure that the playside linebacker is blocked and, if so, continue onto the safety (Diagrams 7-1 and 7-2). The backside guard will also be responsible for any linebacker run-through in the playside A gap. The backside tackle will anchor down the first down lineman in the backside B gap all the way to a 7 technique. If the quarterback checks the play at the line of scrimmage, the scheme will convert to a true veer-in loaded scheme. In that case the backside pulling guard and the playside tackle are responsible for #1 and the first playside inside linebacker who is not in the count (Diagrams 7-3 and 7-4).

Once again, the speed option is designed to turn the corner quickly, taking advantage of defensive players who are charging straight upfield.

CHAPTER 8

The Play-Action Pass

The play-action passing game off the triple-option fake creates opportunities for big plays. These opportunities are a result of defenders overcommitting to the run and disregarding the four quick receivers in the spread offense. The wishbone or flexbone can not create this type of advantage. The intent of the play-action passing game is to make defenders overcommit, or "bite the cheese." These opportunities usually occur later in the game, because early in the game, the coach's words—"play pass first and run second"—are fresh in the defenders' minds. As the game wears on, they become more aggressive and more committed to stopping the run. This creates the opportunity for big plays via the play-action pass.

Quarterback
While faking the inside veer to the right, the quarterback will step to three o'clock, bring the ball through his hip, and hand ride the B-back, moving the ball in the mesh as the B-back runs his track. The quarterback's hand ride of the B-back is an attempt to make defenders overcommit to the play-action fake. He will then step with his left foot down the line to the right and add two additional short choppy steps. Now the quarterback is ready to gain depth off the line by pushing off with his left foot and taking three additional depth steps. The quarterback has to be able to get as much depth as possible and read his keys at the same time. He should end up 4.5 to 5 yards deep, set-up and ready to launch the ball somewhere between the playside hip of the playside guard and the B gap. Sometimes it is necessary for the choppy steps to be at a slight angle to enable the quarterback to gain the additional depth needed to see his read keys. He may also, on certain play-action passing schemes, have an opportunity to stop on a dime and throw the ball to an A-back while he is still on the line of scrimmage. Therefore, a quick release and quick feet are prerequisites for a quarterback in the Spread offense.

B-Back
The B-back will assume his normal three-point stance at a depth of 4.5 to 5 yards. The B-back's role in making defenders "bite the cheese" is as important as the quarterback's. It is imperative that the B-back make the mesh look as much like the triple option as possible. As he runs his track through the mesh, the B-back should roll over the ball, making it appear that he has secured the handoff from the quarterback. He should have the same landmark (the inside leg of the playside guard) as on the triple option. It is important that the B-back not become a blocker until he is past the quarterback's front foot. His basic assignment is the middle linebacker out, knowing that if there is not a middle linebacker there will usually be

a playside B gap linebacker. If no linebacker comes, he will help on the noseguard or the most dangerous down lineman, usually a 2 or 3 technique defender covering the playside guard.

Offensive Line
The playside guard and tackle's main job on the triple-option play action pass is to sell the run. They can not show pass on the snap of the ball. This technique is one of the most difficult for offensive linemen to master. The basic scheme for the playside guard and tackle is White. White means the playside guard blocks the first down lineman over him to the outside. The playside tackle blocks the first down lineman over him to the outside unless the playside guard is uncovered. In that case, he blocks out on the next down lineman to the outside (Diagrams 8-1, 8-2, 8-3, and 8-5). Both the playside guard and the playside tackle sell the run by firing out and popping their assigned defensive linemen. This technique is referred to as a pop and lock technique. The player should fire out and pop the defensive lineman, then come under control and pass protect with his hands inside the framework of the defensive lineman's body. It takes a lot of practice to master this technique, but it is critical to the effectiveness of the play-action passing game off the inside-veer fake.

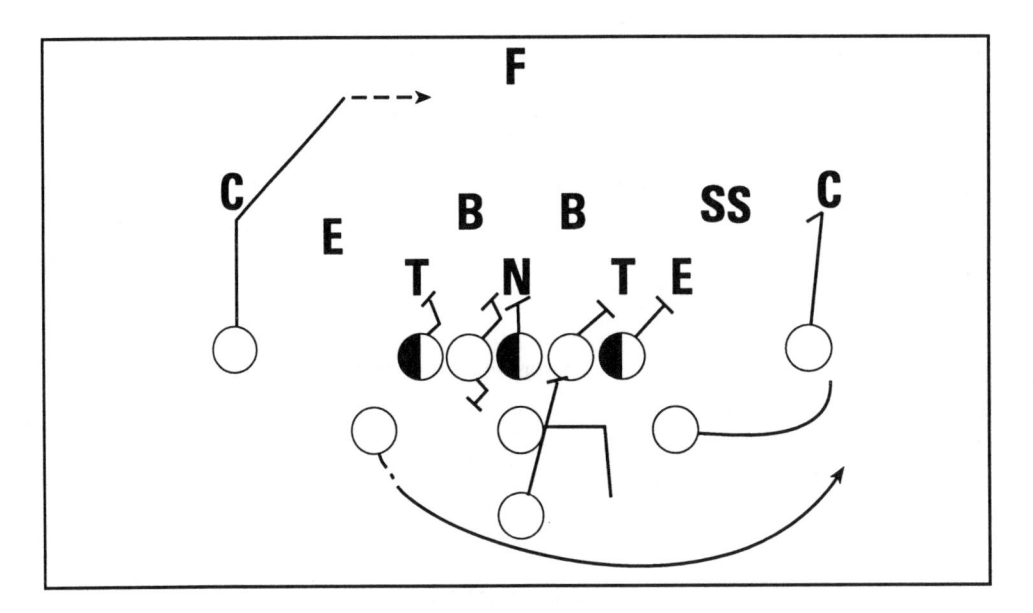

Diagram 8-1

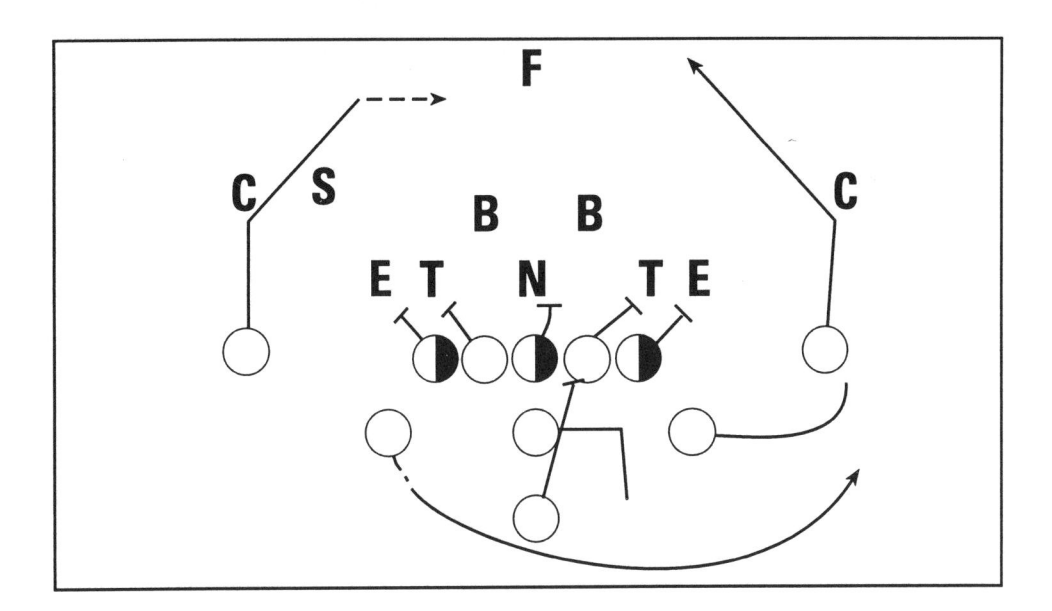

Diagram 8-2

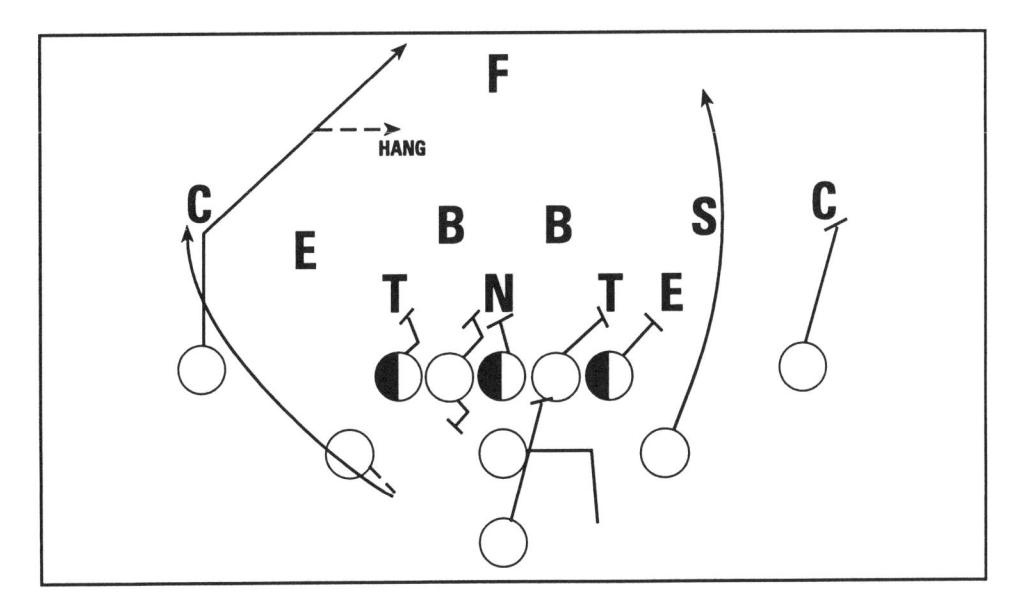

Diagram 8-3

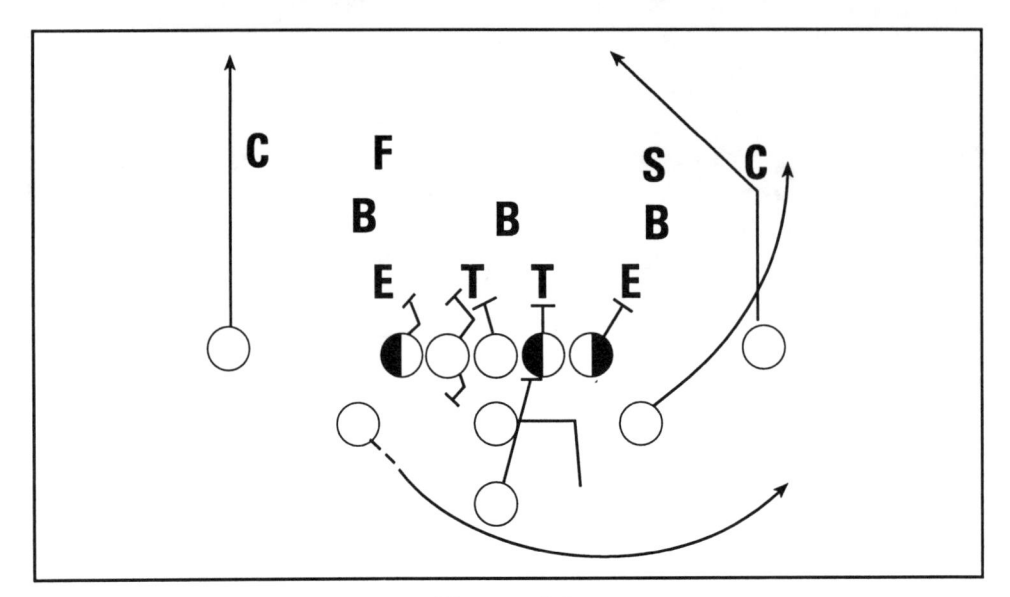

Diagram 8-4

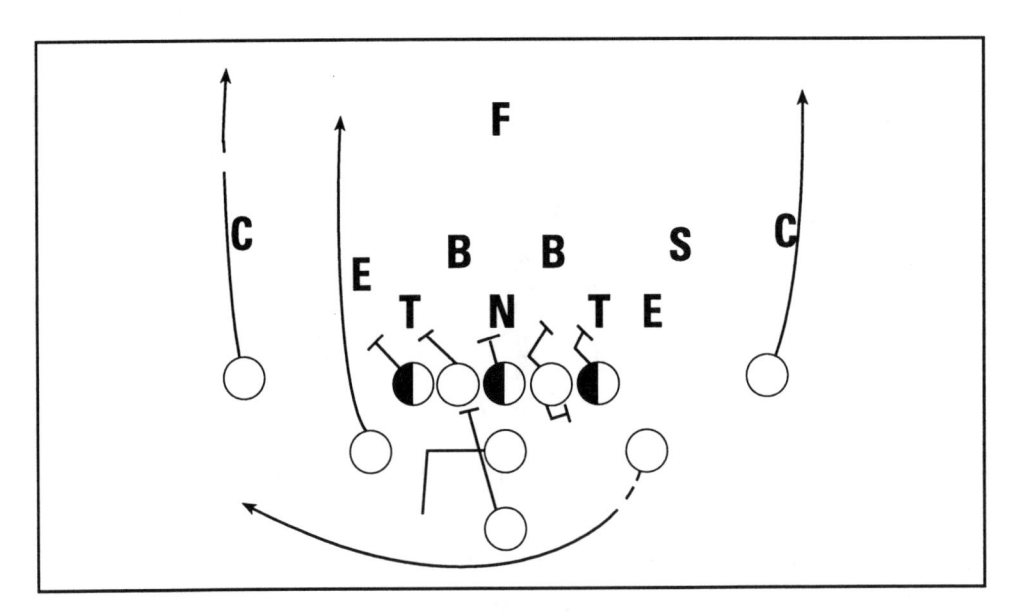

Diagram 8-5

The blocking scheme for the center, backside guard, and backside tackle is called Base Pass Pro. In this scheme they look first in the playside gap, then to the most dangerous defender, then to the backside. If the center has a playside shade, then that defender is the center's responsibility (Diagrams 8-2 and 8-5). This assignment may be the toughest job the center will have in this offense. The center will often get help from the B-back because most defenses will not blitz linebackers against this offense. Also, most teams are currently employing an even-man front without a noseguard, so the center will be uncovered the majority of the time. Nevertheless, if the center has a zero noseguard or a playside shade, he has to snap the ball, take a flat lateral step, and secure pressure with his playside hand on the playside breast plate of the noseguard. The primary objective for the center is to get his arms extended so he can be in control and create separation between himself and the noseguard. If the center is uncovered, he will check the most dangerous linebacker to the backside for a backside edge rusher. If there is not a defender in the playside gap or over him, and there is not a threatening linebacker, then his responsibility is the back door—any defender coming from the backside where the quarterback can not see him. If the center hesitates getting out the back door, the quarterback is in danger of being blind-sided.

The backside guard and tackle use the same rule: playside gap, most dangerous defender, backside, in that order. If the backside guard has a 2i (Diagram 8-6) in his playside gap, then the 2i is his responsibility and he should secure pressure on the playside breastplate of the 2i and cut off the 2I's fastest route to the quarterback's launch point. If he is uncovered (Diagrams 8-1 and 8-3), then he will check the most dangerous backside linebacker to the back door. The same rule applies for the backside tackle.

The backside tackle can make a Four Switch call to take advantage of angles if the backside guard is uncovered (Diagram 8-2). In this case, the backside guard takes the 4i or 4 technique and the backside tackle takes the edge rusher. Another situation the offense must be aware of is referred to as a "dog call" (Diagram 8-6). This call is made by the backside tackle to let the center or backside guard, whichever is responsible for the back door, know that an edge rusher is up on the line of scrimmage and appears to be coming. This call further emphasizes the importance of getting out the back door quickly.

The center can make a you/me call to identify who should take a defensive lineman aligned in the backside A gap. If the center says "me," then he will take the backside A gap defender and the backside guard will check the backside most dangerous linebacker to the back door (Diagram 8-4). If the center says "you," then the backside guard will take the backside A gap defender and the center will check the most dangerous linebacker to the back door. Again, repetitions in practice will make these calls and switching responsibilities second nature to the offensive linemen.

A-Backs and Wideouts

The A-backs and wideouts will use the same alignment as in the normal spread formation. The routes run will be determined by the word tagged at the end of each play-action pass. The backside A-back will go in tail motion prior to the snap of the ball, but will be a secondary receiver. He should flare to the playside, making sure that he remains shallower than the quarterback in order to avoid a potential lateral if he is thrown the ball. The A-backs and wideouts memorize their responsibilities according to the tag word called (see below).

The six basic play-action passes off of the triple-option fake are as follows:

1. Stop
2. Stop X or Z post
3. Switch
4. Switch X or Z post
5. Wheel
6. Vertical

Stop (Diagram 8-1)

The stop route is a common triple-option play pass. The main reason for running a stop route is to keep an inverted strong safety or rolled up corner from disregarding the pass and becoming another linebacker who plays run first and pass second. When an A-back is having trouble arc blocking an inverted strong safety or rolled up corner, it is time to throw the Stop route.

The Stop Route Assignments

Quarterback: The quarterback will hand ride the B-back to his front foot, then take two short choppy steps while reading the flat defender, and staying on line. His progression of receivers is playside wide to flare to backside hang.

Playside A-Back: The playside A-back will sell the run by running his arc track.

Backside A-Back: The backside A-back will run his tail motion, then run flare, making sure he stays shallower than the quarterback.

Playside Wideout: The playside wideout will run an eight-yard stop route, pushing to outside shoulder of defender. If the corner squats, he will try to find a hole between the squat corner and half-field safety.

Backside Wideout: The backside wideout will run the hang route, pushing up the field to a depth of eight yards, then break to a post route to a depth of fourteen yards, then find a hole while working across the field.

Stop X or Z Post (Diagram 8-2)
The play-action playside post, run off of the triple-option fake, is designed to take advantage of an aggressive three-deep free safety. At the beginning of the game the free safety will usually be at normal depth, but as the game progresses he will get closer and closer to the line of scrimmage on his pre-snap alignment. It is natural, regardless of what he has been coached to do during the week, for him to want to get more involved in the running game. This creates an opportunity for a big play by throwing the playside post.

The Stop X or Z Post Assignments
Quarterback: The quarterback will again hand ride the B-back to his front foot, take his short choppy steps, then push off for three depth steps. His receiver progression is read free safety for playside wideout on post to flare A-back to backside hang.

Playside A-Back: The playside A-back will sell the run by running his arc track.

Backside A-Back: The backside A-back will run his tail motion, then run a flare, again making sure he is shallower than the quarterback.

Playside Wideout: The playside wideout pushes the outside shoulder of the corner to a depth of eight yards, then breaks to the post.

Backside Wideout: The backside wideout runs the hang route and pushes upfield to a depth of eight yards, then breaks to the post at a depth of fourteen yards and finds a hole while working across the field.

Switch (Diagram 8-3)
The switch is basically a backside wheel with play action away from the primary receivers. The route developed as a base route because of rotating coverages employed against the Spread offense. Some secondary defenders will start to rotate before the snap of the ball with tail motion. The switch creates an opportunity for big plays by taking advantage of the defensive secondary's tendency to overcompensate on tail motion.

The Switch Route Assignments
Quarterback: The quarterback will again hand ride to his front foot and take his short choppy steps. He will then check the playside A-back, stop set, and throw if the receiver is open. If not, he will push off for three depth steps. His receiver progression is check front side A on line, then read backside wideout to backside A-back.

Playside A-Back: The playside A-back runs vertically, idles, and shows his numbers if he is open at linebacker depth. If not, he will work to the hash to a depth of 18 to 20 yards and idle whenever open.

Backside A-Back: Twirl and work to a depth of 10 to 12 yards, getting no closer than five yards from the sideline, then read the corner. If the corner is deep, the A-back will settle at 10 to 12 yards; if the corner squats, or against man coverage, the A-back continues up the sideline looking for the ball.

Playside Wideout: The playside wideout runs vertically, pushing the outside shoulder of the corner while not getting any closer than five yards from the sideline.

Backside Wideout: The backside wideout runs a post route, first pushing the outside shoulder of the corner to a depth of eight yards, then breaking for the post.

Switch X or Z Hang (Diagram 8-3)

This route is a change of pace to take advantage of underneath coverage playing run first versus the triple-option play action pass. The only change is that the backside wideout will run a hang route. The quarterback will still check the frontside A-back on the line of scrimmage, then take three depth steps and read his progression of backside wideout to backside A-back. This pattern is more of a controlled, high-percentage play pass that will keep the free safety and underneath coverage guessing.

Wheel (Diagram 8-4)

The wheel route came about in the Spread offense as a result of level coverage or four across man. Once again, the defensive secondary will have a tendency to overcommit to the run due to tail motion. The Wheel route and the Switch route are run the same way; however, in Switch the play-action fake is away from the primary receivers, while in Wheel, the play-action fake is to the primary receivers.

The wheel route is an excellent play pass to employ going into the defender's Red Zone (around the 30- to 15-yard line). The defender responsible for forcing from the secondary will often overcommit to the run with the play fake.

The Wheel Route Assignments

Quarterback: The quarterback will hand ride to his front foot, take his short choppy steps, and push off for three depth steps. His receiver progression is playside wideout to playside A-back to backside A-back (flare).

Playside A-Back: The playside A-back will work to a depth of 10 to 12 yards, getting no closer than five yards from the sideline, and read the corner. If the corner is deep, the A-back will settle at 10 to 12 yards; if the corner squats, or against man coverage, the A-back will continue up the sideline looking for ball.

Backside A-Back: The backside A-back will go in tail motion and run flare, making sure he is shallower than the quarterback.

Playside Wideout: The playside wideout will push the outside shoulder of the corner to a depth of eight yards, then break to the post.

Backside Wideout: The backside wideout will run vertically and push the outside shoulder of the corner, not getting any closer than five yards from the sideline, if the corner squats idle in the hole.

Vertical (Diagrams 8-5 and 8-6)
The vertical route is the reason the Spread offense has four quick receivers at the line of scrimmage. The Spread usually dictates a balanced defense and a balanced secondary alignment. Defensive secondary alignments are vulnerable to the play-action pass because they will overcompensate to stop the run. The vertical passing game can be a home run, but it is more often an intermediate play pass, with gains of 15 to 20 yards being the norm.

Vertical Route Assignments
Quarterback: The quarterback will hand ride to his front foot, take his short choppy steps, check the playside A-back, and stop set and throw if the receiver is open. If not, he will push off for three depth steps. Receiver progression is front side A on the line, then playside wideout to playside A-back.

Playside A-Back: The playside A-back runs vertically, idles, and shows his numbers if he is open at linebacker depth. If not, he works to a depth of 18 to 20 yards, finds a hole, and idle.

Backside A-Back: The backside A-back will go in tail motion and run flare, making sure he is shallower than the quarterback.

Playside Wideout: The playside wideout runs vertically and pushes the outside shoulder of the corner, not getting any closer than five yards from the sideline, if the corner squats idle in the hole.

Backside Wideout: The backside wideout runs vertically and pushes the outside shoulder of the corner, not getting any closer than five yards from the sideline, if the corner squats idle in the hole.

CHAPTER 9

Sprint-Out Pass

The sprint-out passing game will highlight the physical abilities of the quarterback in the Spread offense. Once again, the scheme will adhere to the KISS principle. It will not be complicated, but it can be effective through repetition. The objective of the sprint-out passing game is to get on the corner and apply pressure on the defense with a mobile quarterback who has an option to pass or run. It can be argued that sprinting a quarterback rather than using a straight drop-back approach does not force the defense to defend the entire field. This is true to some extent, but the threat of the run or pass option by a mobile quarterback on the corner puts more pressure on a defense than a straight drop-back passing game. Also, the sprint-out passing game is much easier to execute, because the protection scheme does not vary; there are no "hot throws" and no checks versus blitzes.

Trips
The introduction of the sprint-out passing game brings about the need for another formation. This formation is called "Trips" (three receivers to one side of the field) and is shown in Diagrams 9-1 and 9-2. This is not a balanced formation like the Spread, but because of the alignment, it still forces the defense to defend the entire field. Also, many of the same plays introduced in the Spread can be executed from the Trips formation with little or no adjustment. The only major change required to line up in the Trips formation involves the A-back away from the directional call. The designated formation is either Trips Right (Diagram 9-1) or Trips Left (Diagram 9-2). In either case, the A-back away from the directional call will then line up splitting the difference between the playside wide receiver and the A-back aligned next to the offensive tackle.

TRIPS RIGHT

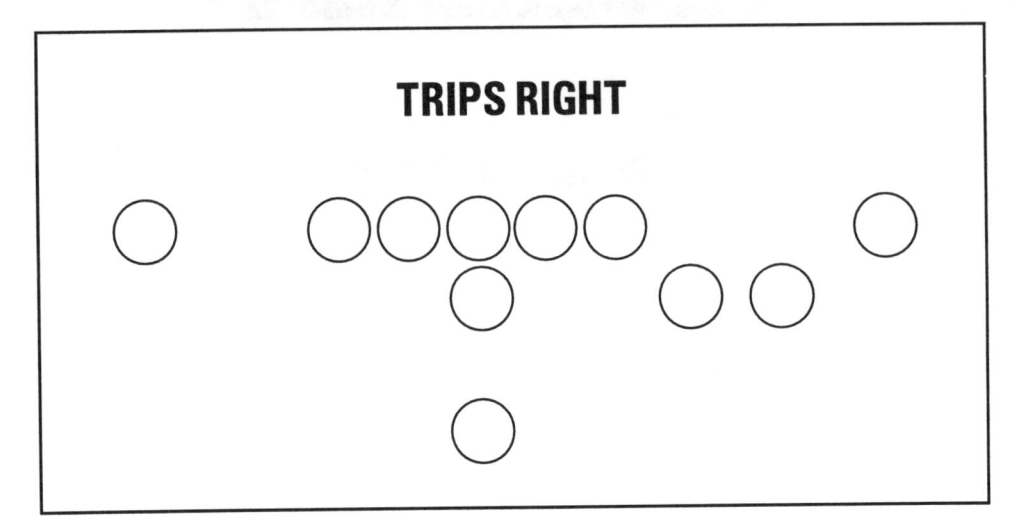

Diagram 9-1

TRIPS LEFT

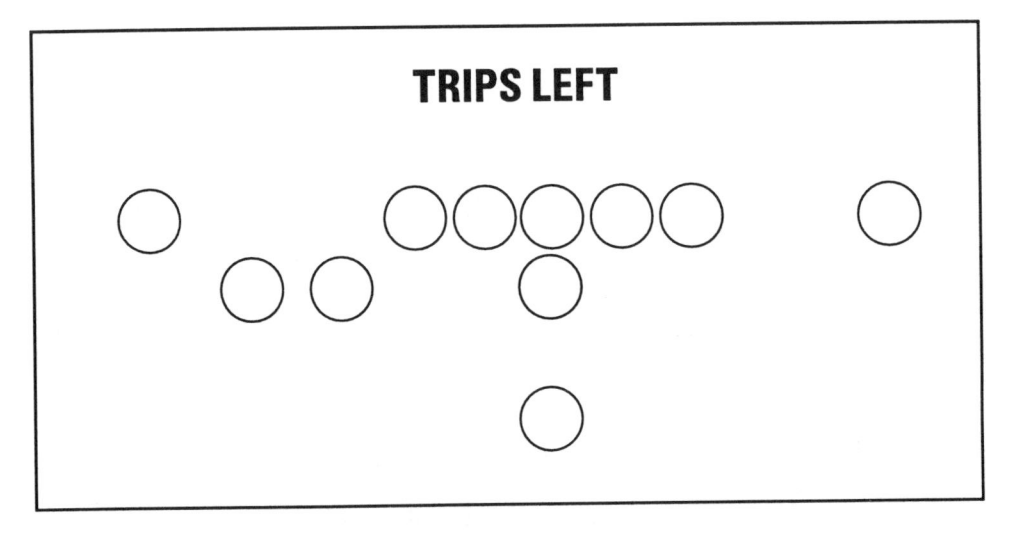

Diagram 9-2

Quarterback

The quarterback, when going to the right, will step to six o'clock with his right foot for depth after he secures the snap from center. On his first step, his left toe will be pointed to the goal line. The second step is a crossover for depth and width at a slight angle. The quarterback will continue working for depth and width until he gets to a point 5.5 to 7 yards deep and to the outside of the B gap. At this point he will have taken five steps for depth and width. The next two steps will be more for width than for depth. At the beginning of the sixth step, the quarterback should start squaring his shoulders to the target as he makes his reads on the run. The ball should be launched as soon as possible after he takes his seventh step for timing purposes. The quarterback should think pass first and break contain to run second.

B-Back
The B-back will assume his three-point stance 4.5 to 5 yards deep. The block of the B-back is critical to the success of the play and increases the quarterback's ability to break contain and have the option to throw or run. The B-back is the second blocker on the corner behind the inside A-back. The B-back's responsibility is to block the first defender who shows up to the outside of the inside A-back's block. When going to the right, the B-back will take a flat step (almost 180 degrees) with his right foot and at the same time focus his eyes on his assignment. He will continue to stay on a flat course, drifting no more than half a yard shallower than his original alignment by the time he is even with the playside tackle's original alignment. At this point he should have a good indication of who he is going to block (usually a defensive end or a scrape linebacker). He will try to secure outside leverage on the defender before he commits himself to going downhill. Once he has secured outside leverage, he will work downhill to cut three inches above the defender's outside knee. He should be trained not to throw his block until he can step on the defender's foot. It is imperative that the B-back get the defender's hands down so the quarterback will have a clear view of his reads and be able to launch the football without a defender in his face.

Inside A-Back
The inside A-back, or the A-back next to the playside offensive tackle, is the first blocker on the corner. He will use the same stance and alignment he uses in the Spread formation. He should get a pre-snap read or a call from the playside offensive tackle to give him an idea what may occur to help him block the first defender who comes into the C gap. This could be a 5 technique, a linebacker scraping in the C gap, or a 4 or 4i technique widening across the playside offensive tackle's face.

The inside A-back will use his normal stance with his inside leg back and his feet shoulder width apart. On the snap of the ball, he will take a short balance step (two to four inches) up the field with his outside foot and then turn in with his shoulders almost perpendicular to the line of scrimmage. His basic responsibility is to block any defender who comes in the C gap or to cut any defender who comes between his nose and the playside offensive tackle's hip. If he tries to stay high with a defender it is often a physical mismatch. He should instead throw or cut three inches above the defender's playside knee and wait to throw until he can step on the defender's foot. There will also be times when defenders will start to threaten the C gap and then try to float across the A-back's face. If this occurs, the A-back will have to adjust on the run by going slightly upfield to carry out his assignment.

Offensive Line
The basic responsibility of the offensive line is to hinge and to block a gap or area that a defender may attempt to penetrate. The technique is the same for all the

offensive line with the exception of a few coaching points. The offensive linemen will use the same stance they have employed in all the previously discussed blocking schemes in the Spread offense. However, for the sprint pass, all offensive linemen will take a short jab step or position step (two to four inches) with their playside foot on the snap of the ball. At the same time they will punch any defensive lineman over them to stop penetration, then they will hinge (drop step with their inside shoulder away from the playside perpendicular to the line of scrimmage). Each offensive lineman's responsibility is to block the first defender who shows up between his nose and the next inside offensive lineman's hip. Once again, there will be times when a defender will start to penetrate a gap and then fight or float across the offensive lineman's face, especially against the playside offensive tackle. In this situation, the playside offensive tackle should lock onto the defensive lineman and the A-back should stay up (above the waist) on any defensive lineman who is in contact with his offensive tackle. This will help the A-back avoid blocking below the waist on a defender while the playside offensive tackle is engaged with the defender at the same time. The backside offensive tackle should block the first defender between him and the sideline. He will have to pass block a speed rusher who is getting up the field and he may have to commit to a defender sooner than the rest of the offensive linemen. If the playside guard, center, or backside guard has a defender who starts to penetrate his gap or area of responsibility, then floats across his face, he can stay with him up to one yard down the field as long as another defender is not threatening his gap. If he tries to stay with the defender more than a yard beyond the line of scrimmage, he is in danger of being an ineligible receiver down field.

One method defenses use to try to disrupt this protection scheme is to attempt to run two defenders through the same gap. Once again, repetition in practice is the best way to teach offensive linemen to handle two defenders attacking in the same gap in game situations.

Outside A-Back and Wideouts
The outside A-back will use the same stance employed in the Spread formation; however, in the Trips formation, he will line up splitting the difference between the playside wideout and the playside offensive tackle's hip. The wideout's stance and alignment will be the same as in the Spread formation. The routes run will be determined by the word tagged at the end of each play called in the huddle, as in the play action passing game. This method requires the outside A-back, playside wideout, and backside wideout to memorize responsibilities according to the tag word called. The three basic sprint-out passes or combination routes off the sprint-out passing game are as follows:

1. Hide
2. Curl
3. Comeback

Hide (Diagrams 9-3 and 9-4)

The Hide route is a combination route that requires the outside A-back to read coverage and adjust on the run. That adjustment makes this combination route a good sprint pass versus a three-deep scheme (Diagram 9-3) or a two-deep scheme (Diagram 9-4). At times other combination routes are better suited for certain coverages or looks, but the Hide route is the one that can be best adapted to almost any coverage or look.

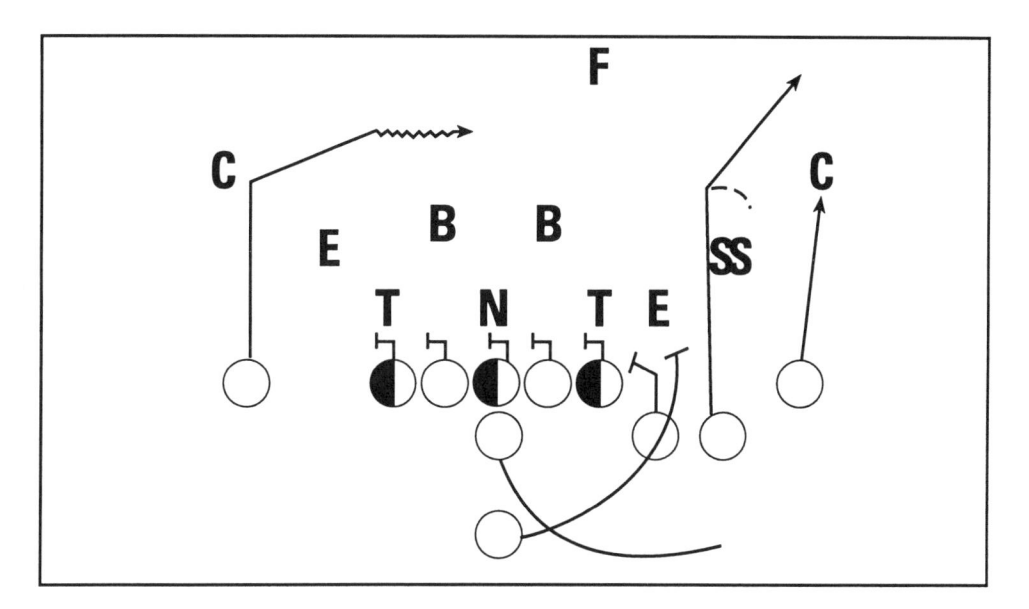

Diagram 9-3

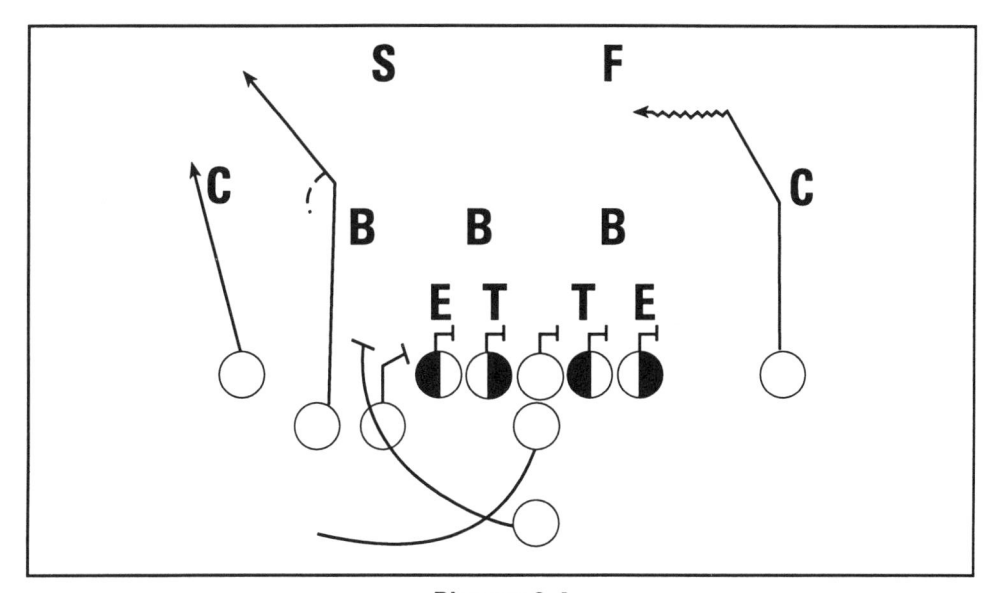

Diagram 9-4

Hide Route Player Assignments

Quarterback: The quarterback should step to six o'clock, crossover, and take five steps to a point 5.5 to 7 yards deep over the B gap. He then takes two steps for width, starting to square his shoulders on the first, and reads the flat defender. His receiver progression is playside wide to outside A-back to run.

Outside A-Back: The outside A-back should go inside the strong safety lined up directly over him, push upfield to a depth of 14 yards, and read and push to the outside shoulder of the near deep safety. He then gives a slight post move and breaks to the corner at 45 degrees. If the near deep safety crosses his face, he turns to the outside hook-up and finds a hole; if the near deep safety does not cross his face he continues on the corner at 45 degrees looking for the ball over his outside shoulder.

Playside Wideout: The playside wideout runs an eight-yard stop route, pushes the outside shoulder of defender while getting no closer than three yards from the sideline, and turns and shows his numbers to the quarterback. He should not convert to the hole versus two deep; if he is covered, he should stay covered.

Backside Wideout: The backside wideout runs a hang route, pushes up the field to a depth of eight yards, breaks to post to a depth of 14 yards, then finds a hole working across the field.

Curl (Diagrams 9-5 and 9-6)

The curl route is the most basic and common route run in all of football. The great thing about the curl is that when executed properly it is still very effective. It is ideally designed to be most effective versus a three-deep coverage (Diagram 9-5), even though it can be run versus two deep (Diagram 9-6). The curl forces an inverted strong safety to make a decision to break on the out or the curl. The important thing to remember is to run the curl wide enough that the playside linebacker responsible for the curl cannot make the play. Also, if the inside A-back and B-back do a good job blocking on the corner, it may force defenses to adjust their coverage by scraping the playside linebacker to help on contain, thus forcing them to assign a different defender to the curl zone.

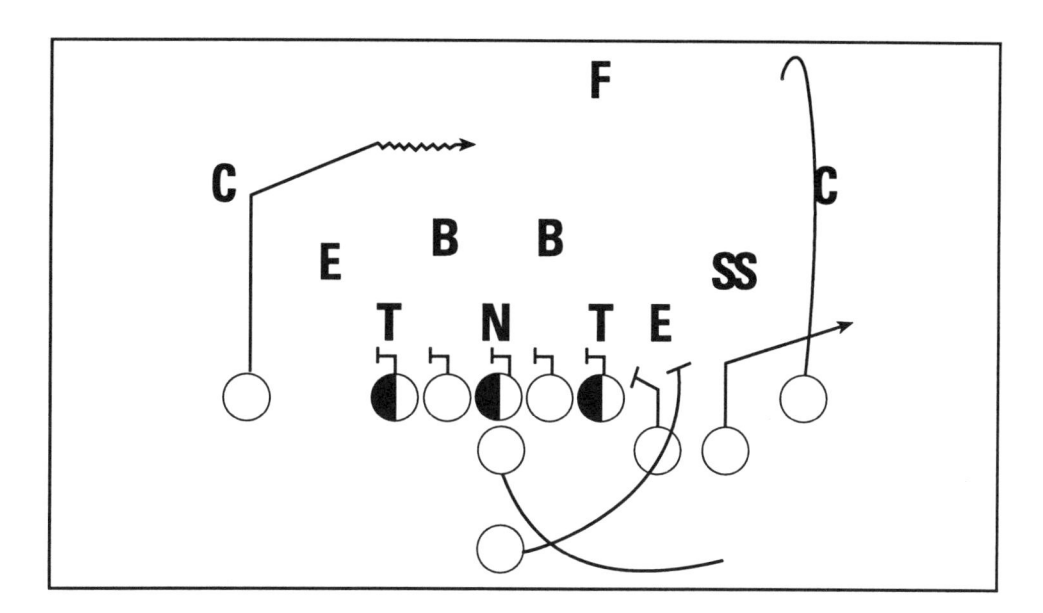

Diagram 9-5

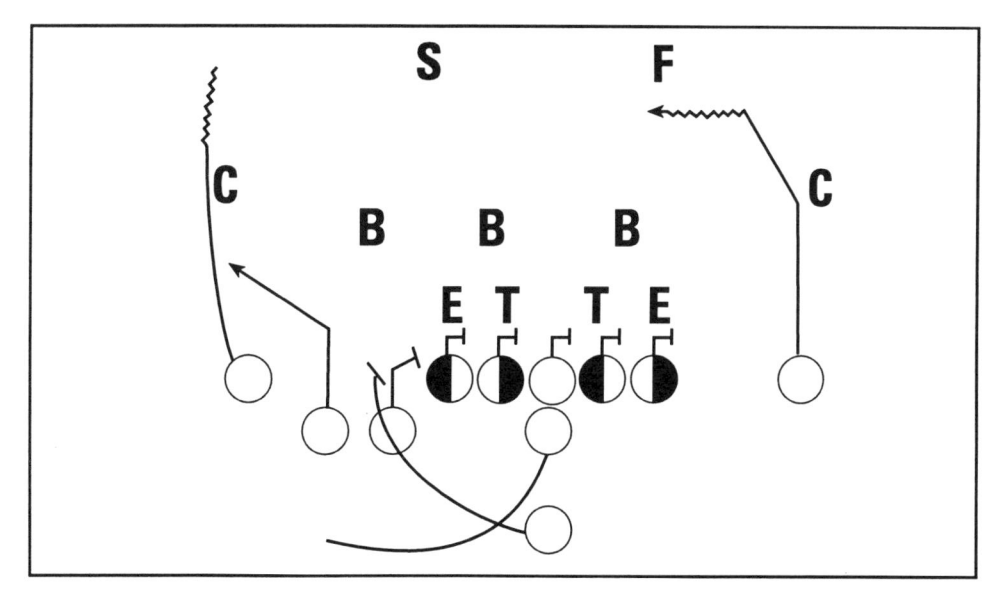

Diagram 9-6

Curl Player Assignments

Quarterback: The quarterback should step to six o'clock, crossover, take five steps to a point 5.5 to 7 yards deep over the B-gap area. He should then take two steps for width, starting to square his shoulders on the first, and read the flat defender. His receiver progression is outside A-back to playside wideout to run.

Outside A-Back: The outside A-back should push up the field for three steps, then break to the flat at an angle that will take him to a depth of seven yards. As soon as he breaks to the flat, he should turn his head to look for the ball.

Playside Wideout: The playside wideout should push straight up the field to a depth of 16 yards, pushing through the outside shoulder of the corner, then turn in and come back two yards to the quarterback. Versus a squat corner or two-deep look he should release outside the corner and idle in the hole underneath the half-field safety and behind the squat corner.

Backside Wideout: The backside wideout runs a hang route, pushing up the field to a depth of eight yards and then breaking to the post to a depth of 14 yards. He then finds a hole while working across the field.

Comeback (Diagrams 9-7 and 9-8)

The comeback route is another common route that has been used by past and current coaches. Once again, some of the most effective pass routes are those that have been in use for many seasons. The comeback route is designed to attack the defender responsible for the flat area and is basically best suited to attack an inverted three-deep strong safety (Diagram 9-7). That is not to say that the comeback can not be run versus two-deep coverage (Diagram 9-8); however, it is a higher percentage throw versus three-deep coverage.

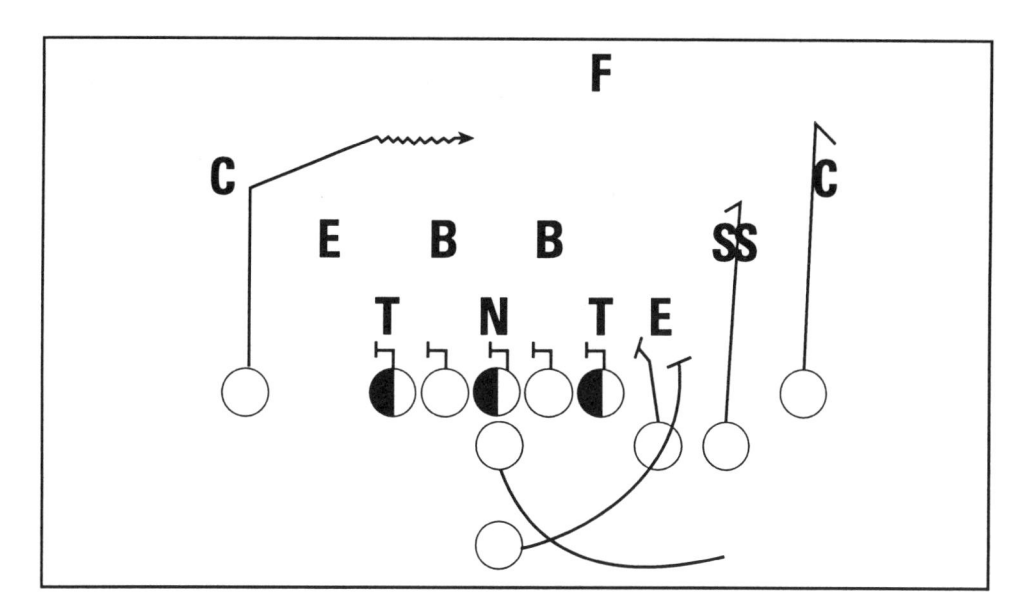

Diagram 9-7

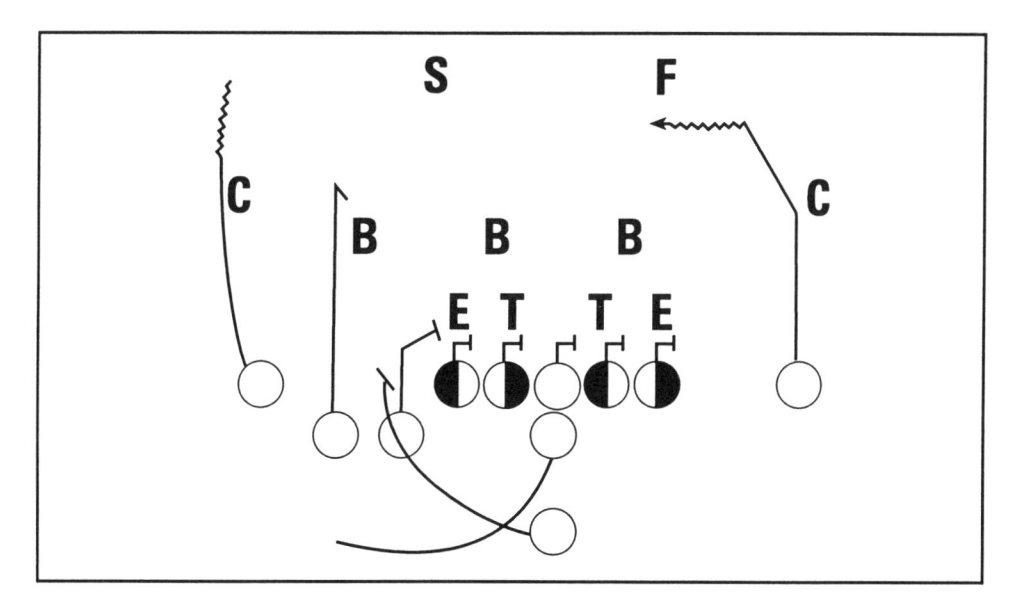

Diagram 9-8

Comeback Player Assignments

Quarterback: The quarterback should step to six o'clock, crossover, and take five steps to a point 5.5 to 7 yards deep over the B-gap. He should then take two steps for width, starting to square his shoulders on the first, and read the flat defender. His receiver progression is outside A-back to playside wideout.

Outside A-Back: The outside A-back should push straight up the field to a depth of eight yards, stop, turn in, and show the quarterback his numbers. Versus a three-deep inverted strong safety he should push through the inside shoulder.

Playside Wideout: The playside wideout should push up the field at the outside shoulder of the corner to a depth of 16 yards, then stop and come back two yards to the sideline at a 45-degree angle. Versus a squat corner or two-deep look, he will release through the outside shoulder of the corner and idle in the hole underneath the half-field safety and behind the squat corner.

Backside Wideout: The backside wideout runs a hang route, pushing up the field to a depth of eight yards, breaking to post to a depth of 14 yards, and then finding a hole while working across the field.

This chapter has presented just a few successful sprint-out passes which have been tested by the Spread and other formations over the years. It is not intended to be a complete list of sprint-out passes, but a rather a foundation on which a coach can build.

CHAPTER 10

Knocking it in the Zone

The toughest three yards in football are the last three before reaching the end zone. This is due to the fact that the field has shrunk to where there is a minimal amount of room in which to run the entire offensive package. Defenses in this area of the field have considerably less ground to cover. Teams have two basic methods to choose from when formulating their goal line offensive packages. One is for the team to line up in a variety of different formations and try to finesse its way into the end zone. The second is to use a simple, straightforward approach and challenge the defense to stop it if they can.

The latter method is the one that will be discussed in this chapter. The team lines up in one formation and runs only one play from that formation. This approach sounds absurd, but it is actually very effective. The formation used is the Power I set with two tight ends, and the play is the loaded-double option off the triple-option fake.

The Power I
The Power I formation is a fantastic alignment from which to run the loaded-double option off the triple fake. To avoid being too wordy in the huddle, the Power I is addressed merely as either Set Right (Diagram 10-1) or Set Left (Diagram 10-2). The word set means there are three backs in the backfield and two tight ends. The directional call (right or left) will designate which side of the I backfield the setback will align on. This play can also be run out of a full house wishbone formation; however, the Power I has two advantages over the full house wishbone: first, a team can always have an opportunity to pitch the ball to its best running back; and second, the position of the setback gives him a better blocking angle on his anticipated assignment. The setback position is usually filled by a team's best blocking A-back or B-back. Since there are not any true tight ends in the Spread offense, these positions will be filled by offensive linemen wearing tight end (80 series) jerseys. This is not essential, but it will help keep defenses honest and force them to respect the pass. A team can accomplish this tight end insertion on the goal line in two ways. One is to designate offensive linemen to wear tight end jerseys and insert them on the goal line. Another method is for the team to carry some 80 series pullover jerseys, and put them on players at appropriate times.

SET RIGHT

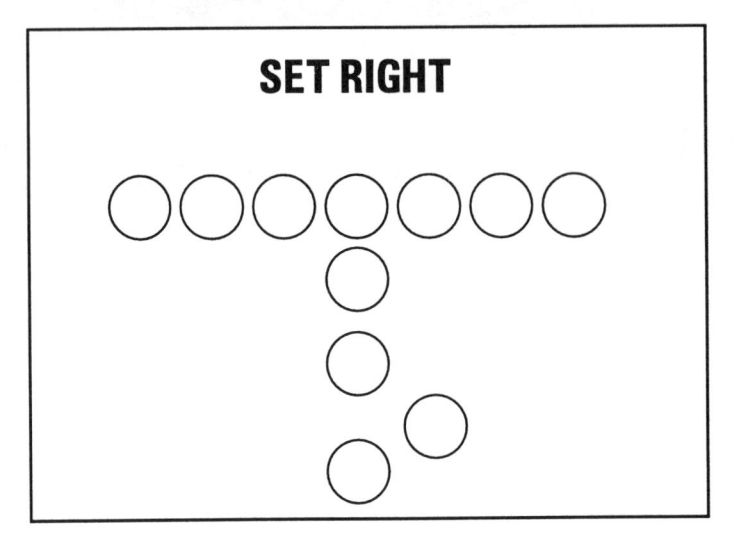

Diagram 10-1

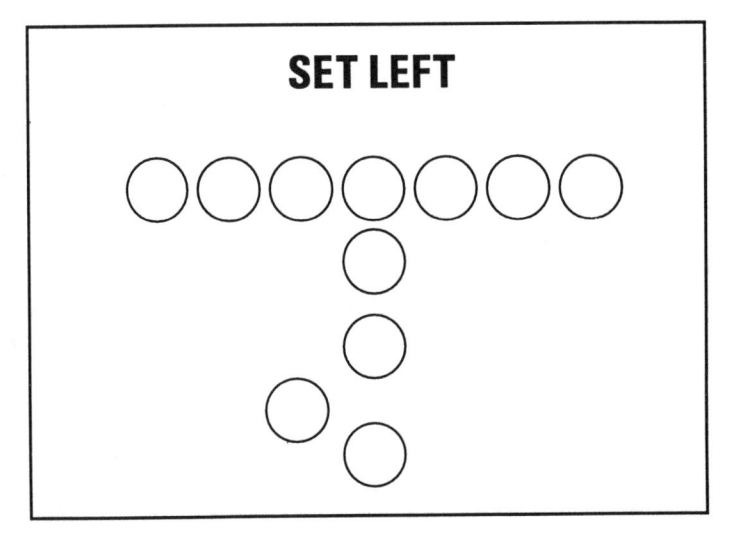

SET LEFT

Diagram 10-2

Quarterback

On the loaded-double option, the quarterback's general rule is to pitch the ball off the cornerback. He will get a pre-snap read to see if the defense has more than one defender aligned outside of either of the tight ends. In this situation, defenders should be counted whether they are on or off the line of scrimmage. If there are two defenders outside of the right tight end's alignment and there is only one defender outside of the left tight end's alignment, the quarterback will check the loaded-double option to the left. If not, he can run the play to the side called.

If there are two defenders outside each tight end's alignment, the quarterback will check "arc" to the side away from the setback's alignment (Diagram 10-6). The setback will go in motion parallel to the line of scrimmage on the rhythmic snap just prior to the snap so he can take a minimum of 1 to 1.5 steps before the ball is snapped. This motion will allow him to get in an optimal position to carry out his arc block on any defender who comes up to provide run support.

On the snap of the ball, the quarterback will step to three o'clock when running the loaded-double option to the right and flash the ball to B-back. As discussed earlier, he will accelerate off the mesh down the line of scrimmage. His assignment is to pitch the ball to the tailback off the playside cornerback. However as he clears the B-back's alignment, the quarterback has the option to run to daylight that opens in the B gap or C gap, or outside the tight end's alignment. He is similar to an I-tailback, except he is not getting the ball as deep in the backfield. Many times the quarterback will follow the B-back or setback up into the B gap or C gap.

B-Back
The B-back's rule is to block the middle linebacker or first available linebacker to the playside from the center out. In other words, if there is not a middle linebacker, he will block the next linebacker out from a middle linebacker's alignment to the playside. On the snap of the ball, the B-back will step with his playside foot at the inside leg of the playside guard. He fakes the mesh with the quarterback and when his second step hits the ground, he can push off to go block his assigned linebacker. It is important that the B-back accelerate from his stance through the mesh to block his assignment. The B-back needs to read on the run and be aware of any run-through linebackers in his area who are trying to get into the backfield and disrupt the play. The B-back should run through the line of scrimmage and cut the playside leg of his assigned linebacker three inches above his playside knee, waiting to throw his block until he can step on the linebacker's foot.

Tailback
The tailback should be the best ball carrier on the perimeter, and preferably the best A-back. He will align 7 to 7.5 yards deep from the front tip of the ball in a two-point stance with his feet shoulder width apart. On the snap of the ball the tailback will open to the playside with his playside foot and run the pitch route. He should stay about five yards from the quarterback's hip, constantly looking at the football for the pitch.

Setback
The setback will align in a normal three-point stance with his grounded hand just behind the heels of the B-back. He will be positioned directly behind the playside guard's alignment. The setback's rule is to block the B gap linebacker out to safety. His aiming point is the outside leg of the playside tackle to the center of the C gap.

On the snap of the ball, the setback will step with his playside foot to his landmark. He will then read the C gap area. If he sees the C gap area open up, he will continue on through the gap looking for a linebacker scraping over the top to the safety (Diagrams 10-3, 10-4, and 10-5). If he sees the C gap close down, he will go just outside the tight end's alignment and look for a linebacker scraping over the top to the safety. Once the setback has identified his assignment, he will cut three inches above the defender's playside leg, throwing his block when he is able to step on the defender's foot. If the play is checked to Arc, then the setback's responsibility is to block run support to the playside. The setback will go in short motion away from his alignment on the rhythmic snap count just prior to the snap (Diagram 10-6). He should be able to take 1 to 1.5 steps before the ball is snapped as he goes parallel to the line of scrimmage away from his alignment. This technique is similar to the timing of a backside A-back going in tail motion prior to the snap of the ball. The setback also has a different responsibility from an A-back blocking run support. The setback is responsible for blocking whoever shows for the pitch. He is blocking an area and will have to read whoever shows for the pitch on the run. The A-back, on the other hand, once he identifies #3, knows he will stay with #3 even if #3 goes to the quarterback rather than the pitch.

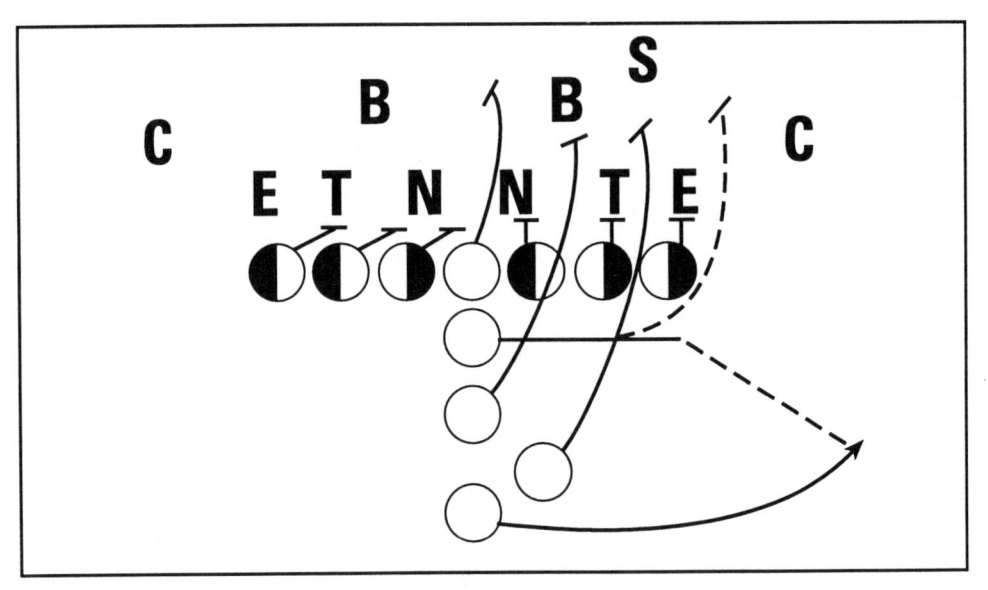

Diagram 10-3

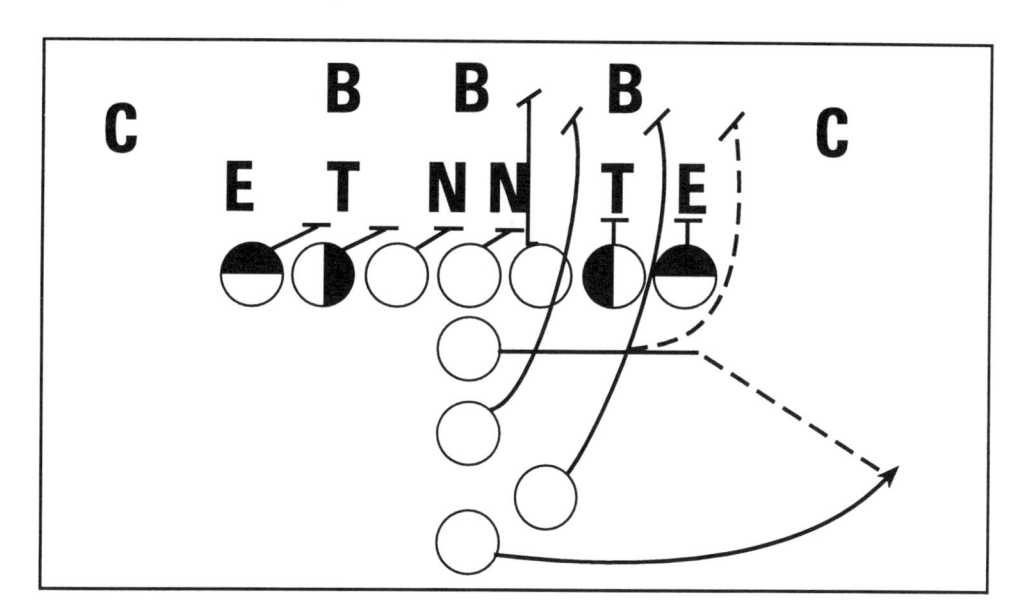

Diagram 10-4

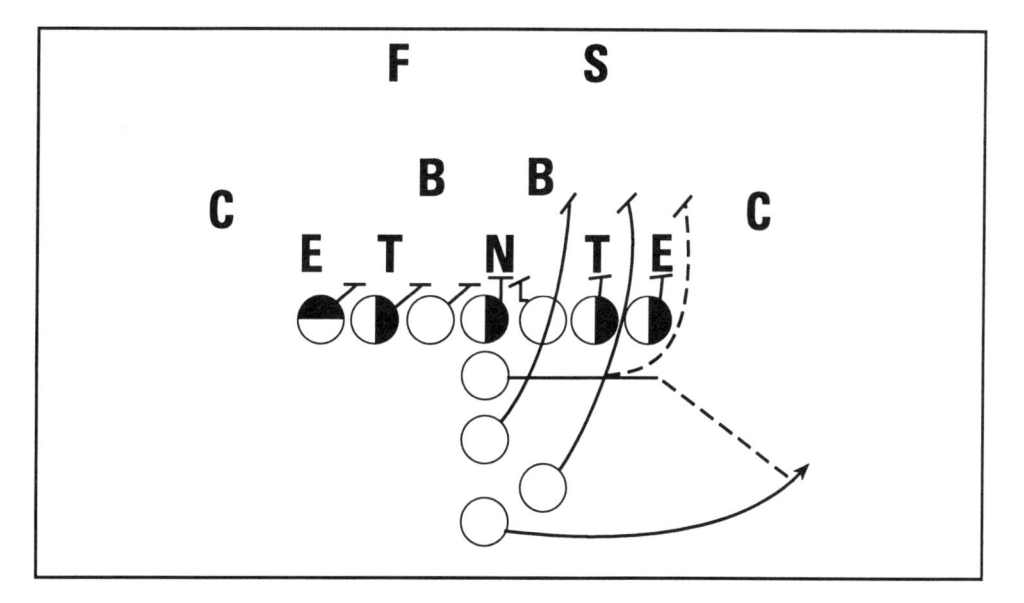

Diagram 10-5

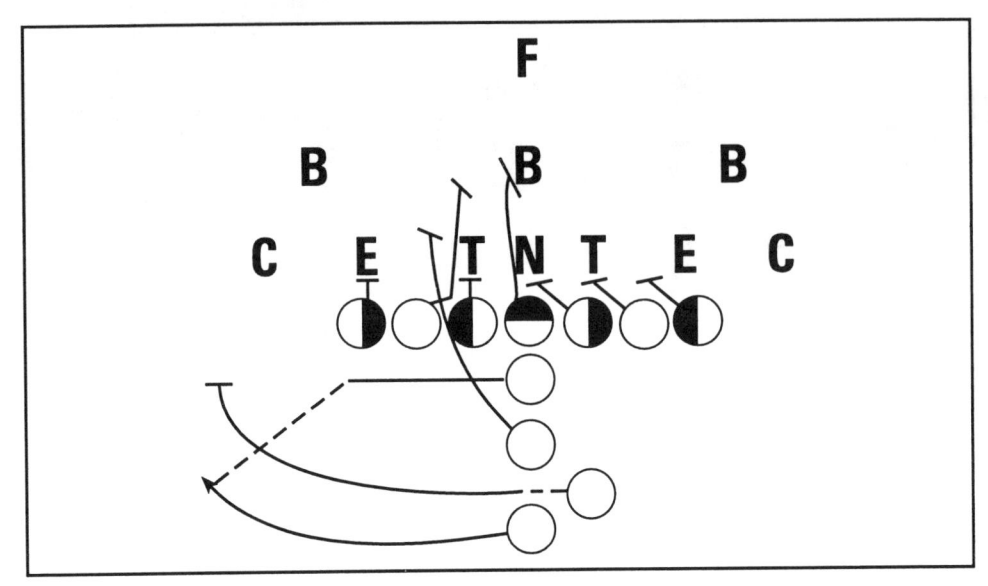

Diagram 10-6

Offensive Line

The offensive linemen will use their normal three-point stance and the three-foot splits until the ball gets to the one-yard line. At that point, the splits will be cut down to one foot all the way across the line of scrimmage. When the ball is on or inside the one-foot line, the splits will be cut down to six inches. It is also important to note that with the ball on or inside the one-yard line, the offensive linemen should align closer to the ball or line of scrimmage. In this area, the advantages of lining up on the center's beltline have virtually disappeared.

Tight Ends

Since there are not any true tight ends in the Spread offense, the tight end positions will be filled with offensive linemen. The primary criteria for the tight ends is that they be able to maintain their blocks. They do not have to be great drive blockers like the guards do in the regular open-field offense.

The playside tight end's rule is to base, meaning inside, over, outside, nearest linebacker. If the playside tight end gets a 9 technique, he will step with his outside foot (Diagrams 10-3 and 10-5). If he gets a 6 or 7 technique over him, then he will step with his inside foot to secure for penetration (Diagrams 10-4 and 10-6). If the playside tight end is uncovered, which rarely happens in the red zone, then he will block the nearest linebacker.

The backside tight end's rule is to scoop, meaning seal the playside gap to the backside linebacker. This scoop technique is no different from the scoop technique employed by the backside guard and tackle in the open-field offense.

The playside guard and tackle's rule is also to base, meaning inside, over, outside, nearest linebacker. In the goal line area, the playside guard and tackle will usually have a down lineman either inside, over, or outside their alignment. However, there are times when the playside guard will be uncovered. If this is the case and there is a playside shade, then the playside guard calls Ace and double teams the shade noseguard with the center (Diagram 10-5). If the playside tackle is uncovered, then he will combo block with the playside guard (Diagram 10-6) by taking a flat step with his inside foot pointing straight up the field through the rib cage to the hip of the down lineman over the playside guard.

The center's rule is to goal-line scoop, meaning he will not be particularly concerned with getting his shoulders flat while securing the playside A gap (Diagram 10-3). He will run a thinner route that will allow him to cut off a middle linebacker or backside scraping linebacker. There is a time in this situation when there will be a down lineman in the center of the playside A gap, which decreases the center's chances of getting out to block a linebacker. If this is the case, then the center has the opportunity to call "Tag," which means the center and playside guard will swap assignments (Diagram 10-4). On the snap of the ball, the center will take a flat step and try to get his left ear on the playside hip of the A gap player. The playside guard will step with his inside foot and rub the playside shoulder pads of the A gap player while he is climbing to the second level to block a middle linebacker or backside scraping linebacker. This technique will allow a lineman to get out on the second level. If no adjustment is made, then the center would probably not be able to get out to block a middle or backside scraping linebacker.

The backside guard, and backside tackle's responsibility is to scoop. This is the same scoop technique they used in the blocking schemes employed in the open-field offense. Scoop means to seal the playside gap to the backside linebacker.

CHAPTER 11

Secondary and Special Plays

There are primary plays a team works on daily at practice that are an integral part of each game plan, and there are secondary plays and special plays. Secondary plays can, at times, develop into primary plays during the course of a season. On the other hand, special plays may not be practiced on a daily basis, and may only be run once or twice a game. The use of special plays depends on the personality development of an offensive attack and the defensive alignments that opponents are employing each week. Sometimes special plays are run only once during a season, or once early in the season and then again late in the season. There are also special plays a team runs not because of the chances of their success but to give opposing defenses something to think about and spend practice time preparing for. If an opponent has to spend 10 minutes preparing to stop each of the three or four special plays a team has in its package, that is 30-40 minutes they can not spend working on defending the triple option. The one secondary play that will be discussed in this chapter is the quarterback draw, and the two special plays will be the reverse off of the triple option and the A-back (halfback) pass off of the triple-option fake. Of course, these plays are not the only secondary or special plays available to a team; however, due to space limitations and a desire to adhere to the KISS principle, they are the three very successful plays which will be discussed here.

The Quarterback Draw (Diagrams 11-1 and 11-2)
The quarterback draw can be run from the Spread or Trips formation. It is an extremely effective play even though there is not a complementary passing game to go along with the quarterback-draw backfield action. The area of the field where it can pay big dividends is from the opponent's 35-yard line to the goal line.

Quarterback Draw Player Assignments
Quarterback: The quarterback draw should be checked by the quarterback to the widest inside technique. For example, if there is a 3 technique on the right and a 2 technique on the left, the quarterback will check the play at the line of scrimmage to the 3 technique side (Diagram 11-2). On the snap of the ball the quarterback will open to the playside and step to five o'clock, then take two additional depth steps before he is able to run to daylight. A lot of quarterbacks, especially young ones, will get in a hurry and either not get enough depth or not take three steps. It is important for the quarterback to remember to take three good depth steps.

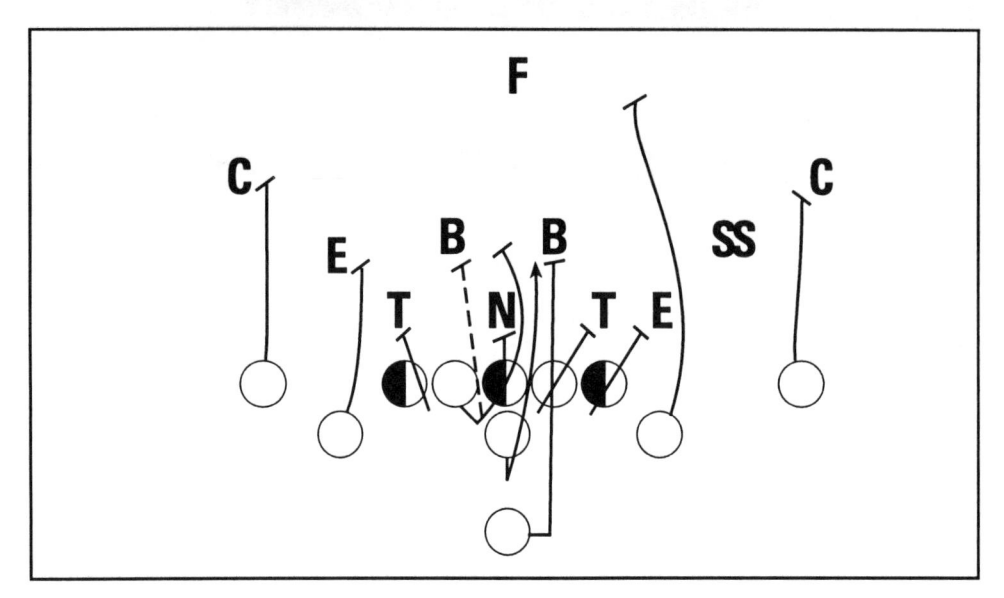

Diagram 11-1

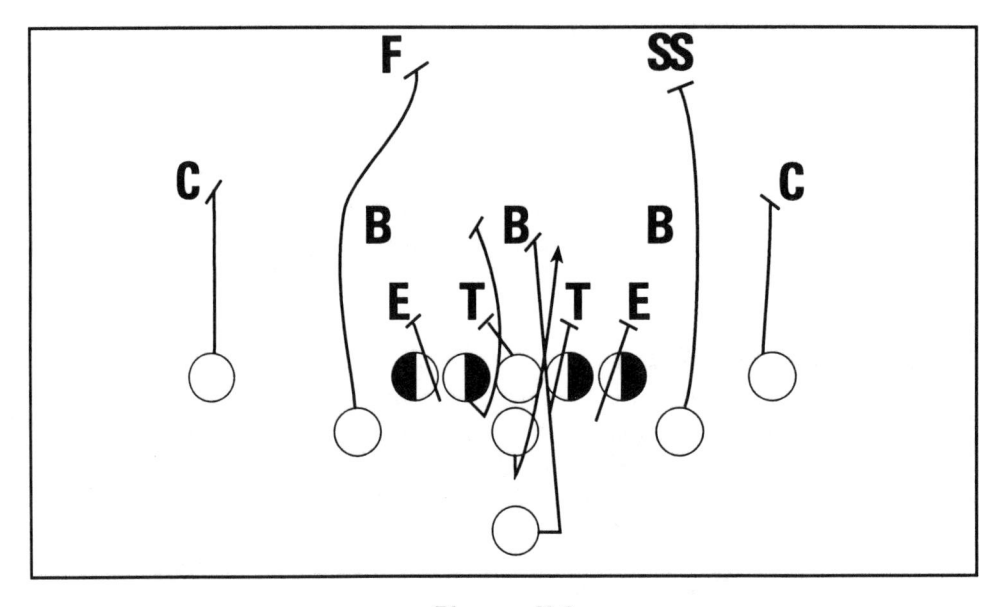

Diagram 11-2

B-Back: The B-back will assume his normal alignment and stance. On the snap of the ball, he will take a short, flat, lateral step with his playside foot, then shuffle with his inside foot first. His assignment is to block the middle linebacker or the first linebacker to the playside from the center out. When the B-back's outside foot off the shuffle (his third step) hits the ground, he will accelerate to block his assigned linebacker. He should throw three inches above the linebacker's playside knee and wait to throw until he can step on the linebacker's foot.

A-Backs: The A-backs will assume their normal two-point stance and alignment. The playside A-back's rule is to block the fold player or near safety, whichever is the most threatening or most dangerous. The backside A-back's rule is to block the near safety unless there is a backside B gap linebacker. If there is a backside B gap linebacker, then the backside A-back will block the fold player.

Wideouts: The wideouts will assume their normal two-point stance and alignment. Both wideouts follow the same rules as they follow on the quarterback draw. They push with a strong release at the inside shoulder of the defensive back over them and then stalk block that same defender. It is important to remember that the quarterback draw can break anywhere, so it is imperative that the wideouts do a good job of turning and positioning themselves between the defender and the ball carrier.

Offensive Line: The offensive linemen will assume their normal stance, splits, and alignment. The playside guard and playside tackle's blocking assignment is to show pass and White, meaning they block the first down lineman over them to the outside. White is the same blocking scheme that the playside guard and playside tackle used on the playside of the triple-option play pass. For the quarterback draw they use the same scheme to identify their assignments, but employ a different blocking technique. They show pass on the snap of the ball and drop step with their inside foot, then do the same with their outside foot. When their outside foot hits the ground, they then attack with both hands.

The aiming point for their attack is the armpit away from where the defender is rushing. For example, if the defender over the playside guard is a 3 technique, he will most likely be a B gap rusher. In this case, the inside armpit of the 3 technique will be the armpit the playside guard will attack and apply pressure to.

As on the backside of play-action pass, the playside guard and tackle can also call a switch to improve their blocking angles. When the playside tackle has a 4 or 4i defender and the playside guard is uncovered (Diagram 11-1), the tackle should call "4 switch." This will give the playside tackle and playside guard the best blocking angles for the guard on the 4 or 4i and the tackle on the rush end or 6 technique.

The center, backside guard, and backside tackle have the same assignment: base to fold. Base tells them who to block, meaning inside, over, outside, nearest linebacker. It is important to remember that any middle linebacker is considered to be a playside linebacker. The backside guard and backside tackle will employ the same technique as the playside guard and playside tackle. The center will still apply pressure to the armpit away from where the defender is rushing, but because he is closer to the line of scrimmage, the center will not have time to drop step. However all three will have the option to call "fold" if the defensive alignment dictates it.

Fold means that the lineman closest to the ball will block back on a down lineman, and the next offensive lineman out will drop step and take the most advantageous route to block the backside linebacker. If the center is covered by a backside shade or 1 technique and the backside guard is uncovered, then the center will block back on the backside shade and the backside guard will drop step and take the most advantageous route to block the backside linebacker (Diagram 11-1).

Another example of a situation when the offensive line would fold would be when the center is uncovered and the backside guard is covered by a 2i technique. The center would then block back on the 2i and the backside guard would drop step and take the most advantageous route to go block the backside linebacker (Diagram 11-2). The same could be true for the backside tackle if he is covered by a 4i technique and the backside guard is uncovered by a down lineman. The backside tackle and backside guard could fold so that better blocking angles can be utilized.

It is important that the offensive lineman, with the exception of the center, stay high, take the defenders where they want to go, and take two good drop steps before they attack the arm pit away from where the defender is rushing.

The Reverse (Diagrams 11-3 and 11-4)
The reverse, run off of the triple option, has always been a good play; however, it is now an even better play because of the increased usage of the 4-3 defense. The 4-3 defensive scheme puts added pressure on the backside defensive end or 5 technique. By alignment, the 5 technique in the base 4-3 scheme has the backside contain responsibility and reverse responsibility. This is a play that defenses are aware of, and they work on containing it, but it is difficult to teach the backside 5 technique to "stay at home" for an entire football game. Much like the play-action pass, as the game goes on, the defender responsible for the reverse forgets what the defensive coaches stressed in practice and becomes too aggressive. When he tries to close on the run or chase the quarterback down from behind on the triple option, a team can run the reverse back at him.

The reverse should be run to the best open field runner playing X or Z. A team can also sometimes get away with subbing for or switching an A-back with the appropriate wideout. Nevertheless, when the quarterback is being chased hard by the backside defensive end or 5 technique, it is time to run the reverse.

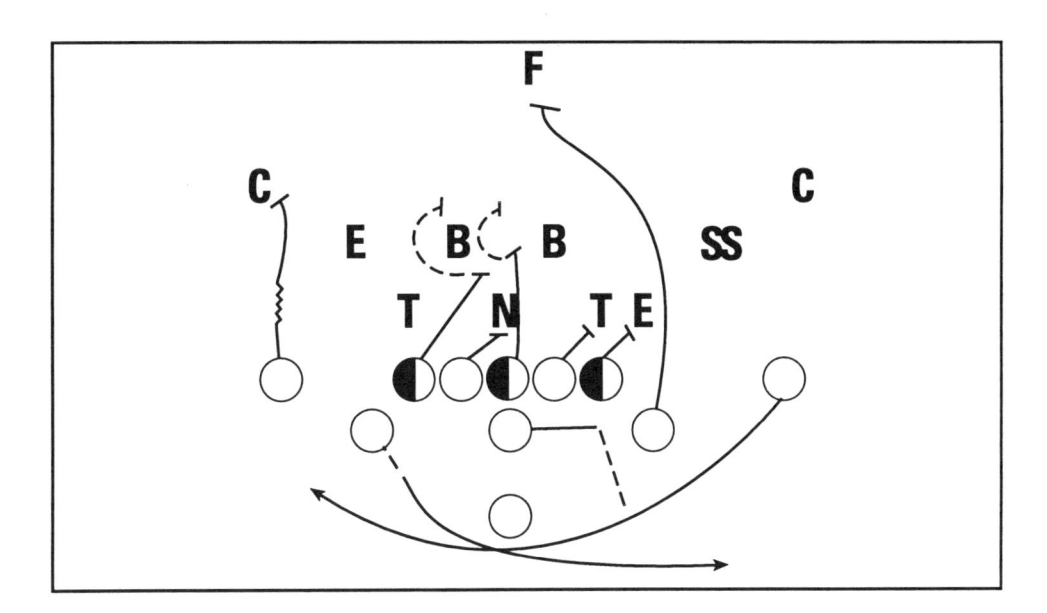

Diagram 11-3

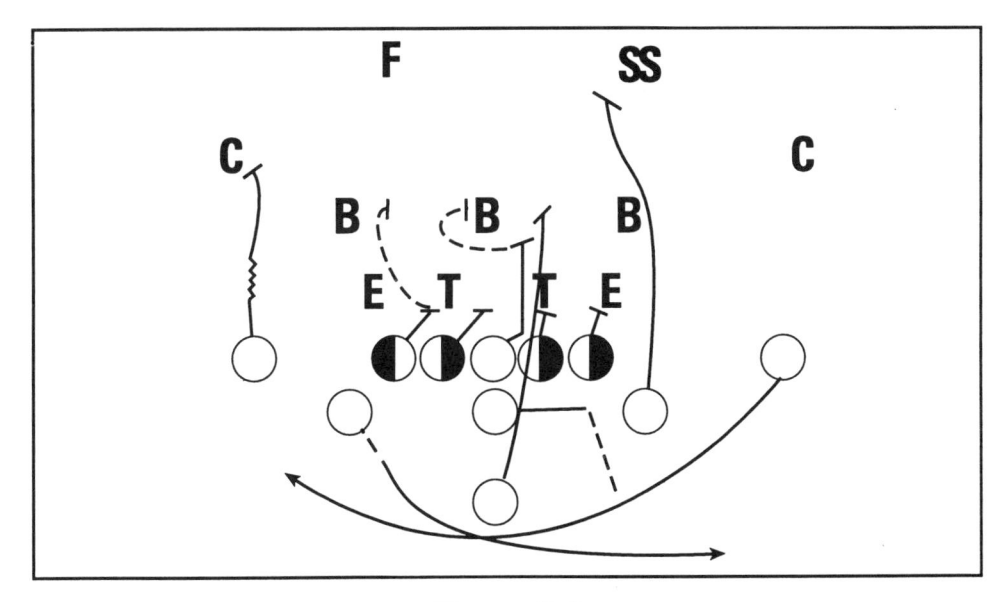

Diagram 11-4

85

The Reverse Player Assignments

Quarterback: The quarterback will open away from the playside and carry out the steps and mechanics used with the triple option. He will step to three o'clock and fake the mesh read with the B-back. The quarterback will go down the line of scrimmage and soft pitch to the wide receiver running the reverse. The quarterback should check to the triple option if there is a hard #2 threatening from the backside. If there is no threatening defender, then the reverse can be run.

B-Back: The B-back will fake the mesh with the quarterback. As he does on the triple option, the B-back will step with his inside foot at the inside leg of the playside guard, and when his second step or inside foot hits the ground, he can push off toward the line of scrimmage. The B-back's responsibility is to block the middle linebacker out to the playside linebacker to the safety.

A-Backs: The playside A-back will go in tail motion prior to the snap of the ball as he does on the triple option. He will run his normal track but will go behind or stay deeper than the wide receiver running the reverse. The backside A-back's responsibility is to release straight up the field and block the safety.

Wide Receivers: On the snap of the ball the backside wide receiver will step with his inside foot and run the reverse route through the heels of the B-back's alignment, which is 4.5 to 5 yards deep. Depending on where the ball is being snapped from, he should get the soft pitch from the quarterback somewhere in the vicinity of the backside offensive tackle's alignment. The playside wide receiver will execute a lazy release and seal the corner after he recognizes the reverse. This is a key block because it takes a considerable amount of time for the reverse to get to the playside perimeter.

Offensive Line: The backside guard and backside tackle will White and sell the run with the same technique used on the playside of the play-action pass. Each blocks the first down lineman over him to the outside. The one exception to the White rule is when the backside guard is uncovered and the backside tackle is covered. The backside guard will then block out on the down lineman over the backside tackle and the backside tackle will block out on the next down lineman to the outside.

The center, playside guard, and playside tackle will scoop to peel. They execute their normal scoop technique and sell the run first. Once they have run their appropriate scoop route, they then peel back out to the playside and block any defender who attempts to cross their face.

The A-Back (Halfback) Pass (Diagrams 11-5 and 11-6)

It seems that almost every offense has the half back pass in its offensive package. This pass is usually run off a team's favorite running play. The Spread attack is not any different; however, it calls the halfback pass the A-back pass. The A-back pass off the triple-option fake is an annual or biannual play; if it is run much more than twice a year, it will lose its effectiveness.

The A-back pass is a play that should be run, whether it works or not, to help keep extremely aggressive secondaries honest. Most offensive plays are designed to score touchdowns. The A-back pass off the triple option is designed to go for the home run. If executed properly, it can have an immediate impact on the momentum of a football game. The pass route employed will be the front side post by the playside wide receiver.

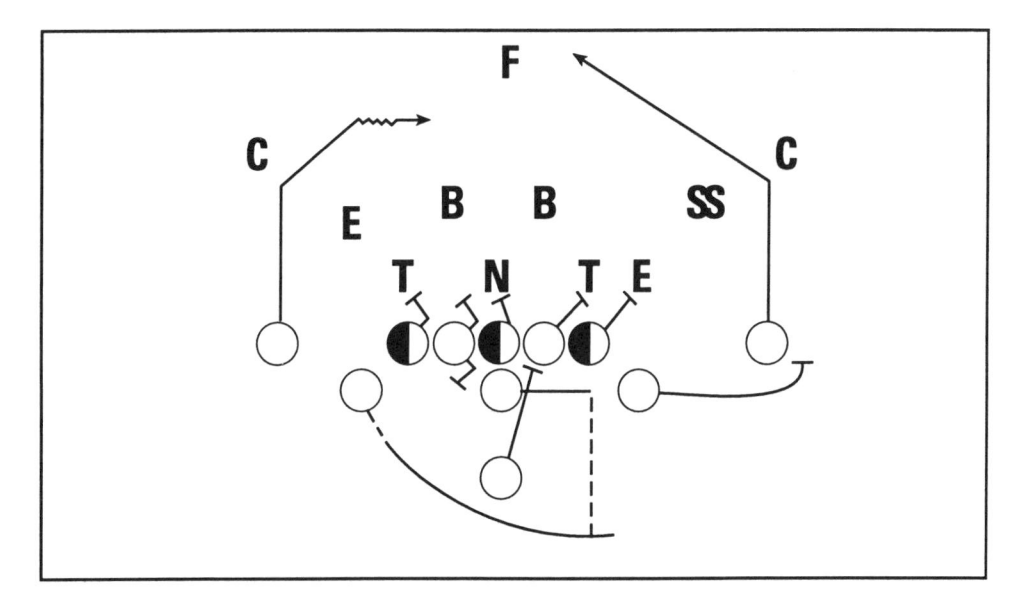

Diagram 11-5

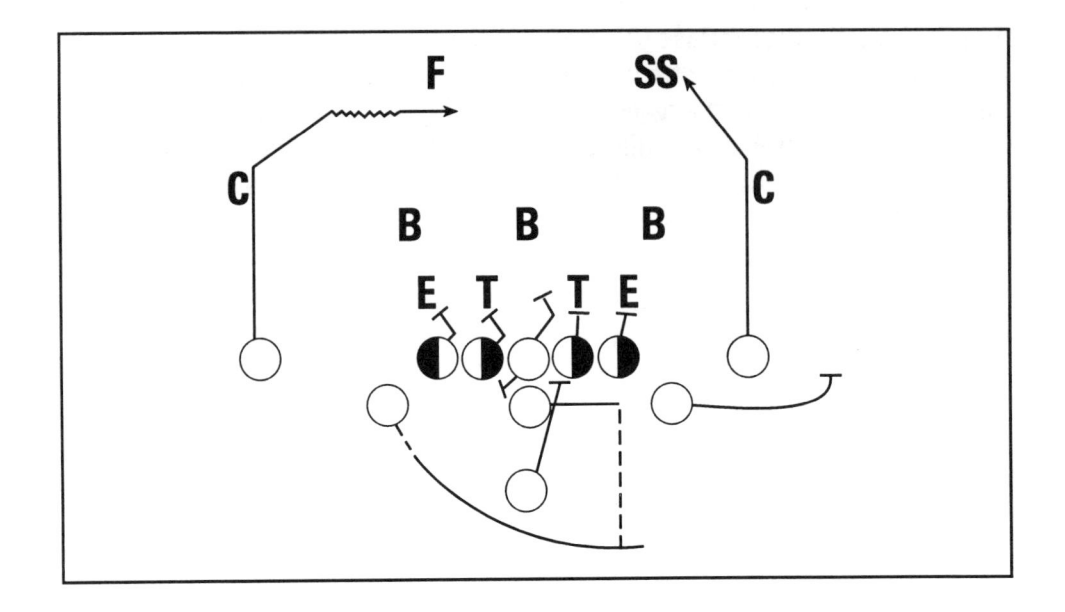

A-Back Pass Player Assignments

Quarterback: The quarterback will step to three o'clock with his playside foot and fake the triple option mesh with the B-back. After faking the mesh, he will continue down the line of scrimmage and then pitch the football to the backside A-back, who is running his normal pitch track. The quarterback will pitch the ball somewhere beyond the alignment of the playside tackle's inside foot (Diagram 11-5). If the quarterback does not accelerate down the line of scrimmage for at least two or three steps, the run fake will not be sufficient enough to make the secondary overcommit to the run.

B-Back: The B-back will run the normal mesh track that he executes on the triple option. It is important for him to run at least two to three feet past the quarterback's front foot before he becomes a blocker. The B-back's responsibility is to block the middle linebacker out to the playside linebacker if they come. If neither linebacker attacks, the B-back can help ensure the center to the playside guard's block.

A-Backs: The playside A-back will run his arc track to help sell the run. This should increase the chances of the playside corner or strong safety overcommitting to the run. At the same time, the arc track can enhance the chances of the free safety overcommitting to the run, making it more advantageous for the post to be open. The backside A-back will go in tail motion prior to the snap and continue to run his normal pitch route through the heels of the B-back. The backside A-back will receive the pitch from the quarterback and tuck the ball away as if he is going to continue running the pitch phase of the triple option. Once he has secured the football with his hands on the laces, he should stop, plant, and throw the post to the playside wideout. It is imperative that he launch the football as soon as possible for his own protection and also because the playside wide will outrun the flight of the ball.

Wide Receivers: The playside wide receiver will assume his normal stance and alignment. On the snap of the ball, the playside wideout will run a post route. He will push straight up the field at the outside shoulder of the corner to a depth of eight yards and then break to the post. The backside wide receiver will run a hang route. He will push straight up the field to a depth of eight yards, break to the post, and at a depth of fourteen yards work across the field and find a hole. It is not very likely that the backside A-back would have the time or experience to look for the secondary receiver or hang route. The hang route is the complementary route of choice because it also has a chance to occupy the safety. Nevertheless, the backside A-back does have a secondary receiver to go to if the post is covered and time permits. Some coaches may not give the backside A-back an option to throw to a secondary receiver in order to keep from making a bad play worse. These coaches should instruct the backside A-back to tuck the ball and get positive yardage if the post is not open.

Offensive Line : The offensive linemen will assume the same stance and alignment they normally do in the open field attack. The pass protection blocking scheme will be the same one that is used for the play-action pass. Once again, the playside guard and tackle's responsibility is White. They block the first down lineman over them to the outside. If the playside guard is uncovered, then the guard will block out on the down lineman over the playside tackle and the playside tackle will block out on the next down lineman to his outside. They will both be aggressive, sell the run, and pop and lock. This will further enhance the chance of the secondary overcommitting to the run.

The center, backside guard, and backside tackle's responsibility is to base pass pro just as they did on the backside of the play-action pass. They look to the playside gap, then the most dangerous defender, and then the backside.

Once again, these are only a few of the special plays that can be added to an offensive package. These plays have two advantages: first, they give a team a chance to score the "home run;" and second, they make opponents spend a considerable amount of time and effort preparing for the fact that they may be run.

CHAPTER 12

Football Graffiti

Some people collect stamps, some sports memorabilia, some antique cars, but this coach collects football graffiti. This last chapter is designed to give the reader some food for thought about coaching, overcoming adversity, achieving goals, leadership, and anything else that might give a coach a mental edge over his opponents. Coaches are constantly searching for a physical or mental advantage. One never knows when a certain cliché, quote, or saying may apply to the situation at hand. Following are some of those thoughts.

Leadership
According to Don Phillips' "Lincoln on Leadership" lecture during the 1996 American Football Coaches Association (AFCA) Conference, Abraham Lincoln defined leadership as three distinct things.

First, a successful leader has *compassion for his people*. A football coach has to have compassion for his players and coaching staff. They should know that he cares about them as individuals. When the players and staff feel this sense of compassion, they will go to any extreme for the good of the cause.

Next, a true leader has a *passion for his work*. The head football coach should have a passion for the greatest team sport on earth, the game of football. Coaching is far from an eight-to-five job. The head football coach has to have "a bad case of the wants" 24 hours a day, 365 days a year in order for his team to be the very best it can be. His passion for the game should be a constant in his everyday life.

Finally, a great leader has to *take action*. If a coach knows something needs to be done and a tough decision has to be made for the good of the team, he should take action and make what he believes is the best decision. If he does not take decisive action, the program will deteriorate and someone else will have his job.

Attitude
The only true disability a coach can have is a bad attitude. It does not matter if he is not the smartest coach in the world or if his team is not the most talented. The most important thing a person can possess is a positive attitude which will help overcome the ups and downs of a football season and everyday life. When a coach has a constant positive attitude, that attitude is contagious to the staff members

and players around him. The team and staff become infected and their positive attitude becomes a force, with everyone involved working together toward a common goal. Once this change takes place, not only will opponents have to defeat the team on the playing field, but they also have to defeat the mental attitude that the team and staff have developed.

Rising Every Time You Fall
One of the greatest tests in life is not never falling, but instead rising every time you do fall. Overcoming adversity is a fact of life and of football. During the course of an individual's life, he will reach high peaks and fall into low valleys, often due to circumstances beyond his control. The same can be said of a football team. The key point is to expound on the positive rather than dwell on the negative. Even the darkest night does not block out all the stars. Some people see a glass of water and say it is half empty; others say it is half full. Teams or individuals can be either eternal optimists or eternal pessimists. Impossible situations are actually brilliantly disguised opportunities. Pressure brings out the true character of an individual or team. How a team or individual responds to adversity will have a direct effect on the outcome of a game, season, or life. Championship teams apply pressure rather than respond to it.

11 Factorial
There are 39,000,000 ways to line up 11 people on defense. Some coaches think the more complex and sophisticated their defensive schemes are, the more effective they will be. In reality, the opposite is true. If a defensive coach gives his defenders too much to think about, the team will be thinking rather than reacting on each play. The defensive schemes employed can have 20 different coverages, 50 different fronts, 30 different stunts, and 25 different blitzes that each player has to master. Instead of being invulnerable, the players will actually not be very good at any scheme employed. If the defensive mastermind will limit his package and gradually work in new schemes, the defenders will be more aggressive and more effective at the same time.

Improvement
Every day a person either gets better or gets worse; he never stays the same. There is no tomorrow, but today is an opportunity to get better and improve. Every day that a coach goes onto the practice field presents an opportunity to be a better coach than he was the day before. This can only be accomplished through preparation off the field. He should have the best practice plans devised in order for his team to be better than they were the day before. The coach should also possess the same desire and demeanor he had the previous day. The individual players and the team as a whole must institute this same approach in order to reach their goals.

Team
Team means being part of something bigger than oneself. Players, coaches, managers, and trainers should all think of the team before themselves. This mentality does not mean a person should not put God first, family second, and the team third; however, once a team has been formed, actions on and off the field should be in the best interest of the team. One example of this concept involves gossip. Proverbs 26: 22 (New International Version) states, "Gossip is a dainty morsel eaten with great relish." Especially in the South, where football is regarded as a religion, people want to know everything that is going on with the high school or college football program. If someone associated with the team adds fuel to the fire of gossip, it is not in the best interest of the team. There have been many times when unfounded, unsubstantiated gossip about the team or an individual team member has caused ill will and loss of focus within a team.

Communication
It is amazing that a message can travel 26,000 miles around the world in less than 1/10 of a second, but sometimes takes years to travel the last 1/8 of an inch. An example of the importance of communication involves the difference in public perception of teachers and coaches. If a history teacher has one student fail the course, the blame is usually placed on the student for not absorbing the material. It is rarely assumed that the teacher did a poor job communicating the course material. The coach, on the other hand, is held responsible for the performance of his players on the field. If the starting quarterback has a bad day and throws five interceptions, the perception is often that the coach did not do an adequate job of coaching. The public's view is that the coach is ultimately responsible for those five interceptions and his team's loss. The coach is held responsible for communicating and making the message travel the last 1/8 of an inch from the tympanic membrane to the autistic nerve and register in the player's brain.

5 P's
Prior Planning Prevents Poor Performance. A coach should have a plan for everything that may occur in a football game. The public may criticize the coach for his play calling on a critical two-point conversion, but few people realize a good football coach had decided on and had his team practice that play earlier in the week. If a strange series of events necessitates playing the third-string quarterback due to injuries, the coach should have a plan for that situation to give the substitute the best chance to lead his team to victory. Good coaches have a plan for everything.

Discipline
If a person does not ask for something, he is not going to get it. If a coach demands that his team be on time to practice, the result will be team punctuality. Players still want and adhere to a structured environment. Creating a structured environment does not mean the coach should be a micromanager. Coaches should worry about

the things that matter. If it is not going to make a difference between winning and losing or affect whether a student-athlete graduates, it should not be the coach's priority. A coach should demand that his players play hard on every play from the time the ball is snapped until the whistle blows. A coach should demand that his players be responsible for their own actions both on and off the field. The coach should not be responsible for knowing how many chin straps, pairs of socks, and rolls of tape are left for the remainder of the season. One of the most difficult things to teach youth is the art of being responsible.

The Press
A coach does not have to answer every question, but he should be available for every question. The best approach to dealing with the media is honesty and availability. If the media senses that a coach is not being truthful, there will always be a sense of mistrust in that relationship. On the other hand, the coach should not be expected to answer every question asked. There have been numerous altercations between coaches and members of the media. It is important to remember that the reporters also have a job to do, and the majority of them want to report the facts. A coach should expect to be criticized; it comes with the territory. However, he should try to avoid confrontations with the media, or too much of his time will be spent trying to win arguments or repair his image.

Fourth and One
Some of the most difficult decisions in coaching football are made on fourth down with one yard to go for the first down or the touchdown. Once again, the decision has most likely been made long before kickoff. The question is not what play to call but whether to call the play at all. Risks have to be taken and gutsy calls have to be made. The most difficult thing to decide is not what may be gained but rather what may be lost.

Six Things That Make a Difference in Football Games
As a football game wears on, the intensity and level of contact wear on opposing teams just as in a heavyweight prize fight. As the fight continues into the later rounds, the contact usually wears down one of the fighters more than the other. In the end, the fighter who has maintained his intensity, physical conditioning, and level of contact will generally win the bout. The same is true in a football game. The team that maintains a higher level of contact throughout the game will, more times than not, find a way to win in the fourth quarter. They do not necessarily provide a knockout punch but maintain a certain level of contact which, in the end, has the same effect.

Unnecessary penalties are basically the mark of an undisciplined football team. This ultimately is the head coach's responsibility. The best philosophical illustration of this concept is that no coach or player will ever be worth one yard in penalties assessed against his team. A certain amount of penalties will always occur during the course of a football game or season; however, one unnecessary penalty at a key point in a game may be the critical difference. Penalties are more mental than physical; it is extremely important to cut unnecessary penalties to a minimum.

Many games have been won by the team that performed at an optimal level in the fourth quarter. The two factors that go a long way toward winning in the fourth quarter are conditioning and the team's development of an attitude that claims the fourth quarter as its own.

During the span of a football game there will always be four or five critical situations that contribute to the final outcome. It may be a fourth and one play, a goal line stand, a third and long, or a punt from deep in the team's own end zone. Whatever they are, a team should be prepared for each critical situation that can occur. Good football coaches prepare their teams for those critical situations by working on them in practice. This sends a message to the team about making the play in the critical situations during the game. Over time, the team learns to look forward to, rather than shy away from, pressure situations.

The kicking game is often overlooked, but it makes up about $1/3$ of a game. The key to success in the kicking game is the approach that the coaching staff takes concerning its importance. If a coach finishes two-a-days and does not work on several different phases of the kicking game, then the end result is that the team will feel the kicking game is not as important as offense or defense. On the other hand, if the majority of the kicking game is introduced during the two-a-day sessions, the team is given a sense of its importance. The coach should also work on different phases of the kicking game daily during a 10 to 15 minute session in the middle of practice. This emphasis will instill in the players a feel for the importance of the kicking game.

The football is the most precious commodity on the field. The game is really very simple. The object is to take the ball and keep it from the opponent while advancing it into their end zone. When comparing game statistics, it is important to note that in close football games, when the majority of the statistics are equal, the winning team is often the one with the fewest turnovers. Some turnovers are contact takeaways that may be beyond a team's control, but the majority of fumbles and interceptions are the result of blatant disregard for the basic fundamentals of securing the football. The best way to minimize turnovers is to set a goal of consistently, have fewer turnovers than the opponent, and constantly teach the basic fundamentals of securing the football.

This book has been merely an introduction to the Spread offense. A coach is limited in his variations and adaptations only by his imagination.

AUTHORS

Tim Stowers has been coaching and developing the Spread Offense for over 12 years. During that time he has been associated with four 1-AA National Titles and one Southern Conference Championship. He averaged 8.5 wins per season during his six years as head coach of the Georgia Southern University Eagles and compiled a record of 51-23 overall and 51-18 versus 1-AA opponents. In his first year as head coach, Georgia Southern won the 1990 1-AA national title and Stowers was awarded the prestigious Kodak 1-AA National Coach of the Year Award. When Georgia Southern joined the Southern Conference in 1993, the Eagles won the conference championship and Stowers was named Southern Conference Coach of the Year by his peers and the media. He is the only coach in Eagles football history to have been associated with every championship the school has won. While at Georgia Southern, Stowers coached 21 All-Americans, 21 All-Southern Conference players, one Jacobs Blocking Trophy winner, and one Southern Conference Defensive Player of the Year.

Stowers graduated from Auburn University in 1980 and earned his Master's degree from the school in 1982. He played five different positions during his playing career at Auburn and until recently was the last two-way performer in Auburn football history. From 1981-83 Stowers was a member of the legendary Pat Dye's Auburn staff. He lives in Statesboro, Georgia, with his wife, Gaye, and their children, T.J. and Lee.

Charles Barry Butzer is a retired Army colonel and a West Point graduate, class of 1962. He is currently teaching math and serving as an assistant football and track coach at Lee Senior High School in Sanford, North Carolina.

Butzer has served as an assistant coach at Fort Bragg, North Carolina, and head coach of the 8th Division Pathfinders in Bad Kreuznach, Germany. He also served as the Officer Representative (OR) for Coaches Art Barker and Bobby Ross at the Citadel.

Butzer's last active duty assignment was Deputy Director of Military Instruction under Colonel Robert "Tex" Turner at West Point. While there, he served as OR to the Army team under Coach Jim Young.

Butzer is married to the former Nancy Rumph. They have one son, Scott, who lives with his wife, Angie, and their two children, Emily and Evan, in New Hampshire.